MY DIRTY DOZEN

MY DIRTY DOZEN

12 FAMILY HEROES

ANNE JENNINGS BRAZIL

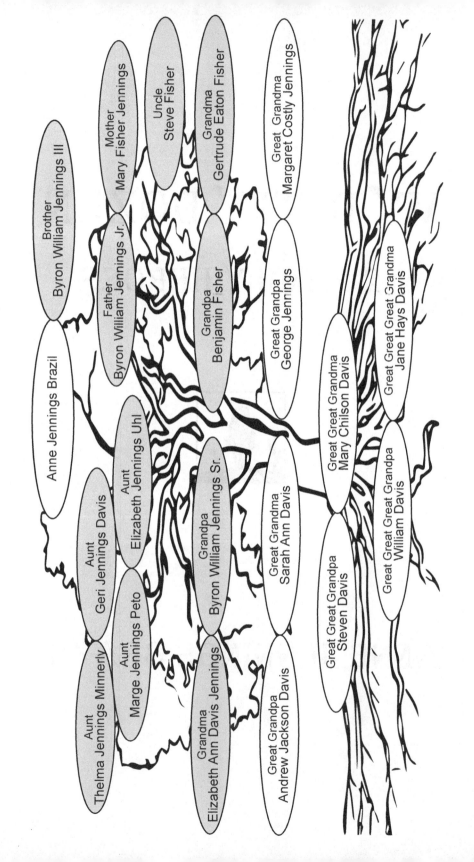

Anne Jennings Brazil	1941-
Brother, Byron William Jennings III	1946-1997
Father, Byron William Jennings Jr.	1911-1984
Aunt Elizabeth Jennings Uhl	1913-1990
Aunt Geri Jennings Davis	1908-1990
Aunt Marge Jennings Peto	1906-1976
Aunt Thelma Jennings Minnerly	1904-1999
Mother, Mary Fisher Jennings	1911-1983
Uncle Steve Fisher	1913-1991
Grandfather Benjamin Fisher	1882-1960
Grandmother Gertrude Eaton Fisher	1889-1985
Grandfather Byron William Jennings Sr.	1870-1955
Great Grandfather George Jennings	1837-1912
Great Grandmother Margaret Costly Jennings	1845-1926
Grandmother Elizabeth Ann Davis Jennings	1872-1913
Great Grandfather Andrew Jackson Davis	1833-1901
Great Grandmother Sarah Ann Davis	1842-1881
Great Great Grandfather Steven Davis	1820-1902
Great Great Grandmother Mary Chilson Davis	1825-
Great Great Great Grandfather William Davis	1794-1832
Great Great Great Grandmother Jane Hays Davis	1794-1832

Dedication

To the twelve pioneers herein

who made me the woman I am today

both by nature and nurture.

Foreword

Through the years I remember hearing compelling stories told, for the most part, by my father and grandfather. Both of them were such colorful characters, I regret I didn't record their tales while they were still with us. Even today there is urgency since it seems I am the last one alive who remembers. My memory, like the negatives in an old shoebox, fades away a little more every day.

I did my best to accurately piece together the rope that connects our family. What I couldn't remember, I researched. Some may be a composite of two or three anecdotes. They may not be entirely factual, and they are not entirely fantasy. They are as close to the truth as I could get.

I became custodian of thousands of family photos. They were enormous help and so meaningful to me; I decided to include an assortment for your pleasure and amusement. Like their subjects, the photos are old. At the same time they harken back to an era when life was simpler, yet required great strength of character.

My family, each one, is a hero in my eyes. This undertaking – remembering them – has caused me to fall in love with them again and again. I hope they do the same for you.

I present these stories to celebrate the uncelebrated. Each character herein is my celebrity, my champion, my star.

Contents

Foreword
Table of Contents
    Indian Creek Massacre   1
1. Grandpa Jennings   15
2. My Father Byron   37
3. Mother Mary   61
4. So So Sewing   85
5. Aunt Liz   91
6. Auntie Marge   107
7. Aunt Geraldine   119
8. Aunt Thelma   127
9. Grandpa Fisher   133
    Fountain Run, KY   147
10. Grandma Fisher   151
11. Uncle Steve   161
12. My Brother Byron   173
Epilogue: A Family of Heroes   207
Quotation: *Dust, Sweat, and Blood*   211
Acknowledgements

Scene of Indian Creek Massacre 1832

Indian Creek Massacre (1832)

The Indian Creek Massacre is a true story. It is a part of American history. On May 20, 1832, at four in the afternoon fifteen settlers were violently murdered by a band of Potawatomi Indians. While seriously traumatized, Sylvia and Rachel Hall along with their brother JW Hall were the only eye-witnesses to report the massacre. I have woven the story from the eye-witness accounts left by the three Hall children. Those were the facts.

The Prairie Davises

My great-great-great-grandfather, William Davis (1794-1832), was a blacksmith by trade, but an explorer by nature. Records show him moving from Kentucky to West Virginia, to Ohio and back to Kentucky in the span of five years. In the spring of 1830 he struck out from Kentucky with his wife and seven children. I wonder what trait in William urged him to attempt such a perilous undertaking. Travel of any distance in those days was strenuous, fraught with pitfalls and danger. There was only room for a minimum of supplies and rations. The trip was more than 400 miles as the crow flies. Crossing rivers, or getting around them, rains, floods, mud, hostile Indians, relentless insects and illness made the trip grueling.

Soon they left Kentucky behind and entered into Illinois territory. They travelled north almost the length of the state. The natural scenery was breathtaking. The prairie was ablaze with spring wild-flowers of every shade as far as the eye could see. They awakened every morning to the dazzling sun as it peeked over the horizon. After a long day's travel they fell asleep to the spectacular light show of the sunset. The pristine scenery made up for the many hardships they suffered. This stunning new territory restored their weary souls.

William Davis took up a claim on the north bank of Indian Creek, on what was to become La Salle County, Illinois. Indian Creek is a tributary of the Fox River and is located sixty miles north-west of Chicago. The river was a much needed resource for their new community. William was the first white settler of the Indian Creek area. Twelve miles away stood Fort Johnson in Ottawa which provided a few supplies, support, and safety in this wild country.

The Davises got by on wild game and berries, until they could erect a saw mill and a blacksmith's shop necessary to survive long term. The saw mill was situated right on Indian Creek. The water flow was fundamental to the operation of the mill. First, William felled trees and devised a primitive dam across the river in order to raise the water level. Next, he constructed a wooden flume or trough to transport the water from the river to his hand-made water wheel. The motion of the wheel operated the machinery created to saw logs. Finally, he built his blacksmith shop next to the house.

Flume brought water from the river to the mill wheel

Soon three families, the Pettigrews, the Hendersons, and the Halls followed and started farms on adjoining tracts. I wonder how the Davises had communicated with these families to join them. The first Pony Express did not come for forty years, in 1860. There was no railroad at all in the State of Illinois until 1836. Some travelled up the river to larger towns and civilization, but river travel was rare and went only to the north. The Pettigrews, Halls, and Hendersons were back in Kentucky to the south. Eventually the message reached them, and the three families made the arduous trip and joined the Davises. This larger community meant more workers, more food, and more protection.

Breaking sod was one of the great challenges of early pioneers. Prairie sod was the top layer of dirt composed of dried foliage of many generations of grasses. The roots were tightly woven into a matted mass up to five miles wide. My grandfather's plows were made for turning soft forest soils and were not able to cut through the brick-like prairie sod. This new terrain destroyed grandpa's plows immediately. Thank God he was a blacksmith and able to rescue the scraps and remake those plows.

One determined settler plowing prairie sod

It still took a strong man with a team of oxen about ten days to till an acre of land. Normally the sod was used to cut into large bricks and make houses, thus delaying the planting another year. My people couldn't wait. There is a legend about a man called "Sod Corn Jones." Jones couldn't wait either and cut the sod with an axe and slipped his valuable corn seed in the crack, and crossed his fingers. Miraculously it worked. With the spring rains the corn sprouted to everyone's amazement. The dirt underneath that sod turned out to be dark, rich, and fertile. My family was pleased at that discovery. They sowed buckwheat, turnips and sod corn and within three months produced the first food from their new land.

They delighted in the harvest and enjoyed their first family feast – loaves of hot buckwheat bread, stew with fresh turnips and corn on the cob. I bet Grandpa William was the first Sod-Corn Jones.

The Potawatomi Indians, who lived on the other side of the river, were disturbed by the fact the Davis dam stopped fish from swimming up-stream past their village. The dam threatened a vital food source for the Indian tribe. A young brave, Keewasee, came to Grandpa William asking him to remove the dam. With no common language they must have acted out their concerns. William refused. He made no secret of his disdain for the red man.

Later Keewasee snuck back and attempted to remove some of the logs from the dam. Davis caught him in the act, grabbed a hickory stick, and beat him badly. It would have been better to have killed the brave. It was as if he was beaten like a dog, and it put shame on him and the entire tribe. This event added to the already existing tensions with Indians. Shabbona, the peaceful chief, approached William Davis to warn him of possible hostilities. Davis refused to take the warning seriously and decided not to move to safer ground. He persuaded the other settlers to band together and fight the Indians off if need be.

● ● ●

May 20, 1832

At the house was Mrs. Davis, the four youngest Davis children, Mrs. Hall with her three daughters, and Mr. and Mrs. Pettigrew with their children. Mr. Hall, and Mr. Davis and sons were nearby in the blacksmith shop with two hired hands. Stephen and Alexander Davis were planting corn a half mile away, along with John Henderson, two Hall boys, and Allen Howard, with his son.

Inside the house an impromptu sewing circle was about to commence. Newly arrived Mr. Pettigrew was holding his baby and chatting with the women. Suddenly a band of sixty to seventy Potowatami Indians wearing horrid war paint crashed the fence and rushed the house. Mr. Pettigrew lunged for the door to hold them off, but he was the first to die by an Indian bullet. The savages grabbed the baby and swung him around by the foot, and dashed his brains against a stump.

Hearing the screams, Grandpa and the other men came running from the shop. The mighty Mr. Davis charged in full force to save the day. He was a strong and powerful man, defending himself with the stalk of his gun and his bare hands, but he was sorely outnumbered and went down with a thud. They brutally murdered and scalped William Davis, his wife, and children. Some were scalped, some hearts were cut out and some of the women were hung by their feet and mutilated beyond recognition. The witnesses were unable to recount the grizzliest details. It was unspeakable.

Next some of the workers in the blacksmith's shop came running and were savagely killed as well. The barbaric butchery went on until fifteen in all were killed that sad day.

Four of the men in the shop decided to run for their lives. They dashed, one by one, down the riverbank. One was shot and fell in the water. Another died on the far bank. Two managed to hide on the near riverbank, out of sight, and escaped. One was Mr. Hall and the other my great-great-uncle William, also known as Big Bill.

One of the Indians grabbed the arm of Little Jimmie Davis, aged 6, to take him with them. The youngster ran as fast as his little legs would carry him, but he could not keep up with the fleeing band of Indians. So one of the braves held Jimmie's outstretched arms while another shot him. They left his body for the scavengers.

My Dirty Dozen

The seven farmers out planting corn a half mile away, heard the commotion and made tracks directly to the Fort in Ottawa. They sprinted those twelve miles taking less than an hour. They met up with the escapees from the river on the way. In that group were my great-great-grandfather, Stephen Davis, and his brothers Alexander and William Davis Jr., Big Bill.

Two pretty, young teenage sisters, Rachel Hall, fifteen, and Sylvia Hall, seventeen, were taken prisoner. The girls, who had already been terrorized, were subjected to nine days of torturous travel on horseback and on foot. One morning their captors made a large round clearing and erected tall spears holding the scalps of the girls' loved ones. Other spears held raw human hearts. The Indians began dancing in and around the Hall girls brandishing more spears in their hands. The young girls panicked. They expected to be stabbed to death any moment. As fate would have it, the girls survived. In the meantime John W. Hall, the brother of the prisoners, had been given shelter by the Governor of Illinois. He was able to solicit the help of some generous benefactors and negotiate a ransom for the release of his sisters. After eleven days in captivity, the girls were set free in exchange for $2000, forty horses, blankets, and food.

After their release, both girls were provided with a tract of land and some money as compensation for their ordeal. Within a year each of the Hall girls married. They lived long and fruitful lives in spite of everything. I wonder how they coped with those horrible events etched in their memories. Why were they taken captive you ask? Two of the

Potawatomi braves were in love. Mr. Hall had allowed the braves an occasional visit with his daughters, considering it a joke. That joke probably saved the lives of his girls.

Those were the facts. What I can't report are the feelings, the motivations, and the history of the players in this drama. What happened back in Kentucky, when William was a boy, to put hate in his heart? Did the recent Black Hawk wars make him fearful and defensive? What made Keewasee so volatile? Was he the scapegoat of his tribe? Had he been abused? Did Shabona, who warned Grandpa William, have some good experiences with the white settlers? What made him so sympathetic and wise? It is tempting to pass blame and judgment around and make up in our own minds who the good guys were and who the bad guys were, but we cannot know what someone else has been through. Some say William Davis had it coming. Some say all Indians are savages. It was a different place and a different time. Life was primitive and sometimes brutal. Each person had to figure out how to survive. And survive they did.

Survivor Stephen Davis, my great-great-grandfather, was the father of Sarah Ann Davis, who in turn was the mother of Elizabeth Ann. Lizzie was the mother of Byron Jennings, my father. Great-grandma Sarah Ann Davis married another pioneer, Andrew Jackson Davis, in an area of California known as Farmersville.

Stephen, Sarah, Lizzie and my father were pioneers in their own right and were also survivors. Let's save them for another day.

My Dirty Dozen

*Andrew Jackson Davis, Sarah Ann Davis,
Elizabeth Ann Davis, Andrew Porter Davis*

Andrew Jackson Davis
(1833 – 1901)
Great Grandpa Andy
The Pioneer

Andrew Jackson Davis, father of my grandmother was not from California. He was a native of Tennessee, born there in 1833. At the age of 21 he heard about the California Gold Rush, left home, and headed west to strike it rich in the gold fields. It is likely he took the well-worn California Trail over the Sierra Nevadas. There was no railroad at the time, no stage lines, or Pony Express. It was a long, hard, hot, dirty trip, and many died en-route. He didn't arrive in San Francisco until the spring of the next year, 1855.

Once he regrouped he headed east toward Placerville to pan for gold on Webber Creek, a feeder to the American River. That was the second most popular gold mine just behind the famous Sutter's Mill. Placerville had been called Hangtown in the past. Hangtown got its name for good reason. A large influx of fortune hunters from around the world attracted unsavory characters who committed robbery and even murder. Vigilante justice was meted out to criminals at the end of a rope, often at the giant oak tree in the center of town.

Andrew moved from town to town along the river to pan for gold. By 1858 the yield of gold became slim pickin's and the flurry of the gold rush had run down. Great grandpa, Andrew moved on south, ending up in the area five miles east of Visalia known as Farmersville, California. While I didn't know him, I have a faint memory of my father referring to his grandfather as *Andy*. I believe he was commonly known as Andy, rather than Andrew.

He homesteaded 160 acres – erecting buildings and cultivating the land. He had one of the finest farms in the area. Coincidentally, Andy met a woman of the same surname, Davis. In time he married Sarah Ann Davis, granddaughter of William Davis of the Indian Creek Massacre fame, bearing no relation to his family. Andy and Sarah had seven children – four boys and three girls. Lizzie, my grandmother, was fifth in line. Of her six siblings, three died in childhood, and two moved away. Only Lizzie and her youngest brother, Andrew Porter Davis, remained near the family homestead and contributed to the community. Andrew Porter Davis developed his own orchards of prunes and peaches adjacent to the home place. Uncle Porter, as my father called him, helped his father work the original homestead along with his own farm, and when Andy died, Porter received 30 acres, his share of the estate.

Meanwhile my grandparents Lizzie and Byron Jennings, were busy establishing their own farm in the area. They had five kids, one of whom was my father, Byron Jennings Jr. He, like his Uncle Porter, remained close by and worked hand in hand with his father. The Davis and the Jennings families established this part of California. They converted virgin soil to highly productive farm land. They were the backbone of the community.

I am a proud descendent of these great pioneers!

Andrew Jackson Davis
(1833 – 1901)

George Jennings   *Margaret Costly Jennings*

1
Byron William Jennings Sr.
(1870 – 1955)
Grandpa Jennings

Byron William Jennings Sr.
in Tulare County Mounted Sheriff's Posse uniform
silver mounted saddle and tack
Ginger, his prized palomino

George and Margaret welcomed their son Byron William Jennings on Valentine's Day, 1870, in Elkport, Iowa. He always told the story that he came from Jawbridge, Kansas, though there seems to be no record of such a place. This tends to make one suspicious of all his family stories, pithy as they were. I put them to paper anyway, in case they might bear some relationship to the truth.

Great grandpa George Jennings' home place, Cherokee, Kansas

Byron was the second of four, three boys and a girl. He was expected to do his share of the farm work, which he didn't mind. What he minded was, as a Seventh Day Adventist, not being able to play with his friends on Saturdays, while his friends could not play on Sundays. He told the story with a wry smile which made us wonder how much truth there was in it. Just like Jawbridge, Kansas, I have not found any corroborating evidence. It is, however, a story that has been repeated around the family table.

The transcontinental railroad reached the west coast in 1869. As a teenager Byron learned Morse code and worked for the railroad in 1884 as a boy-telegrapher. He used these earnings to put himself through normal school in Ft. Scott, Kansas. With his teaching certificate in hand, he went to work as a teacher in Kansas for a short time.

Normal School class in Ft. Scott, Kansas, circa 1885
Byron, front row center

Most likely because the pay was so low, he got a job with the railroad again and worked his way across the country, arriving in Visalia at the ripe old age of seventeen. As a strong and bracing youngster, Byron had no problem fudging on his age and landing a job working in the logging camps of Kaweah and Mineral King.

In four years Byron put himself in a position to become his own boss. He left logging behind and looked for land in Farmersville, east of Visalia. If the future is any indication, he probably purchased no more than thirty or forty acres of virgin soil. He cleared the land of brush and boulders and leveled the acreage. He used only the most primitive tools, oxen, horses, as well as sheer muscle and sweat. Byron most likely planted grain first as it is a winter crop and does well with rain-fall alone.

Byron met and courted a lovely local girl, Elizabeth Ann Davis, who was from a pioneer family in Farmersville. William Davis, of the Indian Creek Massacre, was her great-grand-father. Her given name was Elizabeth Ann, but everyone called her Lizzie. They married in 1891 when Byron was 21 and Lizzie was 19. Byron and Lizzie were prominent citizens of the area, both for their contributions and their heritage. Even as a farm girl, Lizzie helped form the Farmersville Ladies' Club, which provided both social and philanthropic opportunities for its members.

Farmersville Ladies' Club, circa 1890, Lizzie Davis, top row center

Byron and Lizzie Jennings' wedding 1891

Byron was a leader about town. He belonged to the Farm Bureau, the Elks club, The Chamber of Commerce, and later became a charter member of the Tulare County Mounted Sheriff's Posse. Byron and his son, Byron Jr., rode in horse shows and parades on matching palomino horses and silver mounted saddles. Byron also put together a community band in Farmersville. Not only that, he published a newspaper for the area.

Byron on tuba. far left

Byron was a great baseball fan and decided to donate land in the town to be used as a sand lot baseball diamond for the children of Farmersville. Jennings Park is still in existence to this day.

Jennings Park 2015

Elizabeth Ann (Lizzie) – Thelma, left – Madge, front – Geri, top right – Byron Jr., baby

It was almost thirteen years before any children were born. Finally, five kids came, one every two years. Then, sadly, Lizzie passed away at the age of forty. The story was told that one fine day Lizzie walked the long 200 yard lane to the mailbox by the highway. She was excited to discover a package in the mailbox. When she opened it, there was a beautiful negligée. She was devastated to find out that the negligée was not intended for her, but for another woman. In 1913 after a family picnic where she caught a chill in the damp spring grass, Grandma Lizzie lost her battle with pneumonia. Do you think the negligée incident might have caused her to lose her will to live? Some people claimed she died of a broken heart. Anyway she contributed five strong, successful children to the world. That is a lot to celebrate.

Byron never remarried. He raised the four eldest children while Elizabeth at three months, was adopted out to the Ball family in Visalia. She was always considered a full-fledged member of both families.

Byron was well known for the palominos, thoroughbreds, and polo ponies he raised. The palominos were excellent saddle horses and performed in horse shows and parades. The back end of the property had a race track on it. People came from miles around to race and play polo.

Palomino foal

Grandpa Jennings

*Byron with palomino mare
stable in background*

*IBN Grenada 1915
polo stallion*

In about 1945 there was a horrible fire in the stable and most of the horses perished. The disaster put a pall on the whole operation. It was impossible to recover financially or emotionally from such a loss.

My Dirty Dozen

Missouri Jack

Mules were essential to the operation of a farm because a mule is stronger and has more stamina than a horse. They were used constantly to cultivate fields and even orchards. This gave Byron an idea. As you may know, a mule is a hybrid animal created from breeding a mare to a jackass or donkey. You can't breed a mule to a mule. A high quality jack is a valuable commodity. Byron found out somehow that there was an older couple back in Missouri who had a premium jackass as a family pet. He took a trip to visit these sweet, but naïve folks, and before they knew what happened, Byron was heading to California with their pet and they had $3000. The going rate was roughly $5000 for a jack of that quality. He put out the word and soon farmers lined that 200 yard lane with their mares for insemination. He paid no attention to the regulation that a jackass should be bred no more than twice a day. The jack survived, and Grandpa got a pocket full of cash.

He also raised cattle for milk and beef, and hogs for pork. He smoked the beef and pork and stored it in the smokehouse on the premises. They bread, branded, butchered and dehorned right on the property. In order to feed the livestock, he planted alfalfa. The alfalfa had to be mowed, dried, and baled, which could then be stored to feed the horses and cattle through the winter months. Alfalfa, being a summer crop, required irrigation and a nearby water source, such as a small river or ditch.

Byron slopping the hogs

I spent all my time with Daddy, Byron Jr., until I started school. This was one of those early morning outings. It was barely daylight and chilly. Daddy, Grandpa, and the hired hands were congregated near the pig pen pictured above. They had a well-worn wooden frame, maybe ten feet tall, with screw bolts and pulleys at the top. One of the hired hands wrestled a hog from the pen and tied its hind legs to chains affixed to those pulleys. They hoisted the squealing animal until it was suspended helplessly in the air on that wood frame. Someone took a sledge hammer and put it out of its misery with one loud thud. It squirmed and shrieked and finally died. I was taken aback, but when I looked around, nobody else was repulsed or even surprised. I held my feelings in because I didn't want to be sent back to the house. Then Grandpa approached the pig with a huge sharp knife and with one fell swoop ripped his belly from stem to stern. Blood squirted everywhere and the intestines fell on the dirt. While Grandpa completed the cleaning with his expert knife skills, I noticed a cloud of steam coming from the warm animal's body in the cold morning air. It had an unmistakable stench. I was grossed out but resisted reacting whatsoever. This was one powerful lesson. I wanted to be a good girl and go along with the program. I knew what happened when I acted out. I didn't want to be sent back to the house; I didn't want to be left out; I didn't want to be a bad girl; I didn't want to lose my Daddy's love. No book and no lecture could have taken the place of this real life classroom.

Brands were used to identify which ranch grazing livestock belonged to. The Jennings ranch had its own registered brand and branding irons. It was "Quarter Circle J" and it looked like this:

Once clearing, planting and harvesting were in full swing, grandpa could see his way to buy an adjoining piece of land to clear, plant, and harvest. Little by little the Jennings' holdings grew and diversified. He planted prune trees, peach trees, apple trees and walnut trees. He also planted cotton. In order to qualify for a cotton subsidy from the government, he was required to alternate the cotton with cover crops. There were many cover crops throughout the years, such as black eyed peas, iceberg lettuce, and watermelon. Once I was eight or ten, it was my job to sell these crops on the side of the road.

Yokut Indian artifacts

The Yokut Indians were the original owners of the Tule River area. Grandpa Byron and my father, Byron Jr., frequently plowed up Yokut artifacts. There were so many mortar and pestles, utensils, and arrowheads that we paid them no mind.

Grandpa planted a personal orchard of fruit trees right by the house. There were early peaches and late peaches, early apples and late, nectarines, apricots, pomegranates, oranges, grapefruit, lemons, even almonds, pecans, and walnuts. It was so cleverly planned that something was fresh from spring till fall.

Windmill, water tank, and smokehouse

There was a windmill and a water tank near the house. I remember Grandpa climbing that tower in order to fish out a dead raccoon or opossum. The lid must have dislodged from the tank, so the varmit fell in. We bathed in that water and even drank it. If we could survive that water, we could survive most anything.

Byron was a fantastic cook. He could make a pancake the size of a cast iron skillet, an inch thick, and still light as a feather. The memories of his beef roasts make my mouth water to this day, with cloves of garlic stuck all over, a salty crust, rare, juicy, and oh-so-tender. He canned everything he grew. The wood shelves in the cellar were lined with mason jars of everything you can imagine. He had to purchase very little during the winter months.

He knew his way around the making of beer and wine too. A story was told that when he entertained in the living room, sometimes bottles in the cellar went, "pop, pop, pop." This must have been during prohibition, as everyone pretended they heard nothing at all. They just continued to visit as if everything was normal.

Even as a widower, Byron managed to maintain an active social life. He had a model T which was used around the farm. By 1910 Henry Ford improved the production of the first automobile for the masses. One could be purchased for $290. Of course you could order any color you wanted as long as it was black.

Model T

Byron often said, "I have no intention of squiring ladies around in that old Tin Lizzie." He parked his Winton Six touring car at a service station in Visalia, where they kept it shined, gassed-up, and ready to go.

Winton Six

He drove the Model T into Visalia, parked it, and took the Winton Six to Fresno for a night on the town. The Winton Six – 6 cylinders – was *the* luxury vehicle of the day. They were built by hand. The original 1896 model could speed along at 33 mph. In 1902 the Winton Bullet set a record at 70 mph. In 1916 the original price was $2200-$3500 depending on options. Byron must have been proud of that car as it became a family story.

Grandma Carr, a widow, lived a few miles away on another farm. From time to time we took a drive over for a visit. We called her Grandma even though we were not related. We all sat on the porch, and enjoyed lemonade and cookies. This must have happened fairly frequently, as I remember

Grandma Carr quite fondly. Nobody said anything about the nature of their relationship. They acted like friends. If someone dared to ask them why they didn't marry, they would have answered in unison. "There are *nine* reasons: five of his and four of hers." The kids, all of them, were *spirited*. Some said *wild*.

The Panama-Pacific International Exposition, a world's fair celebrating the completion of the Panama Canal, was held in San Francisco, 1915-1916. As a self-made man, Byron took advantage of as many cultural events as possible. It's no surprise that he found a way to take in this chance of a lifetime. He enjoyed many sights and wandered in the direction of the Oregon building. This pavilion displayed natural resources and products of the Pacific North West. One item caught his eye, a mantel piece carved out of solid Oregon apple wood, a work of art, really. Byron wheeled and dealed and was able to purchase that mantel. It was extremely heavy and unwieldy, probably equal in size and weight to a grand piano. How could he get it home? He had it put on the train that took it as far as Fresno, forty miles from home. Then Byron hitched up a team of mules to a big wagon, and step by careful step, brought that mantel home. He had it installed over his fireplace, where it stayed until my father got married. It was then moved to Byron Jr's house, and now it is in my house. That piece has been with me my entire life. What a treasure.

My Dirty Dozen

From Panama-Pacific International Exposition 1915-16

When you live in the country, Halloween takes on a different flavor compared to Halloween for city kids, who cover huge neighborhoods and take home bales of candy. We dressed in an old sheet, and piled in the car to visit maybe half dozen neighbors. Grandpa claimed to be hard of hearing, thus we were always repeating and speaking-up for him. One Halloween we showed up at Grandpa's. The door was never locked, and nobody ever knocked. We always walked right in. One Halloween I wanted to trick my Grandpa. So out of character, I knocked and called out,

"Trick or Treat!, Mr. Jennings!"… (long silence)…

(from inside) "What?"

"Trick or Treat, Mr. Jennings!" I repeated, snickering quietly.

(again from inside). "Oh come on in, Anne!"

I so wanted to fool him, but the joke was on me. The homemade treats were no less sweet, nor is this precious memory.

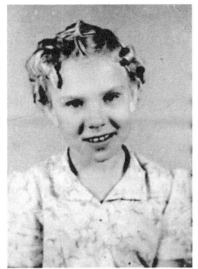

Doris McDaniel, about age 9 *Doris McDaniel*

Many of my early years were spent on a horse. My life-long friend, Doris McDaniel, saddled up Pal, and rode through the orchards to our place where she helped me get my horse, Sugar, ready to ride. We had many escapades. Often we ventured down that 200 yard lane to Grandpa's house. He always had cold Seven-Up™ and grenadine on hand, and a package of store-bought ginger snaps. During the sizzling summer months in The Valley, a cold drink and cookies were so refreshing in the shade of the porch on that squeaky old glider.

Unlike most adults, Grandpa did not demand that kids be seen and not heard. We discussed issues of the day. I remember being shocked that he wanted to hear my opinion. He listened attentively to my ideas, and took me seriously. That old man, with a simple human exchange, instilled in me a strong sense of self that remains to this very day.

It was a well-lived life. Byron William Jennings played it close to the edge, and took advantage of opportunities as they came his way. He did not shy away from hard work, and he knew how to get the most out of those who worked for him. His son, Byron Jr., called him "the great psychologist." It was not an easy life, but it was rich: Rich in experiences, rich in people, rich in accomplishment. He cleverly took his humble beginnings, and converted them into a fruitful life. Byron enjoyed 85 years on this earth, and he made a difference. He was well-liked and well-loved, and because of Byron, the world is a better place.

Byron William Jennings
1870-1955

Grandpa Jennings

Byron W. Jennings, 85, Pioneer Local Rancher, Dies In Exeter Hospital

Byron William Jennings, pioneer Visalia district rancher, died yesterday afternoon in the Exeter Memorial Hospital, where he had been a patient for the last two and one-half weeks.

The old-time Tulare County resident, who came to this area as a boy of 17, observed his 85th birthday last February.

He had been active until about a month ago, when he went to visit a daughter in North Carlsbad, Calif. He was there for two weeks and then was removed to the Exeter hospital, where he was one of the first six patients admitted to the new Boswell Convalescent Wing.

Widely known throughout the county and the state, Mr. Jennings lived for nearly 65 years on his ranch east of Visalia. He was well known as a breeder of horses and for his interest in sports.

Mr. Jennings was born Feb. 14, 1870, in Elkport, Ia., a son of the late George and Margaret Jennings, who came to the United States from London. He spent his boyhood in the midwest, attending normal school at Ft. Scott, Kan. He worked on the railroad as a boy as a telegrapher in order to finance his education.

After being graduated from the normal school, he taught school in Kansas for a short time before starting west, working for the railroad. He worked on the Royal Gorge run of the Denver and Rio Grande prior to arriving in Visalia in 1887, where he went to work in logging camps in the mountains.

In 1891, he and Elizabeth Ann Davis, member of a pioneer Farmersville family, were married, and they settled down on the present Jennings ranch east of Visalia. In his early farming days, he did grain farming, then later converted his acreage into orchards.

For many years, Mr. Jennings bred thoroughbred horses and polo ponies. In his later years, his interests turned to Palominos.

He was a charter member and organizer of the Tulare County Sheriff's Posse, although he has been inactive in that group for several years.

Always interested in community development, Mr. Jennings helped to organize a band in Farmersville, and was instrumental in the organization of baseball teams there. At one time, he published a newspaper there.

He maintained an active interest in the Visalia professional baseball team and attended games whenever he could.

He was a long-time member of the Visalia Elks Lodge, the county chamber of commerce, and the Tulare County Farm Bureau.

Mr. Jennings is survived by four daughters and one son, Thelma Jennings Farrar of Subic Bay, Philippine Islands, Marjorie J. Peto, N. Carlsbad, Geraldine J. Davis, Beaver Lodge, Alberta, Canada, Elizabeth Ball Uhl, Visalia, and Byron William Jennings Jr. of Visalia.

Other survivors include a sister, Mrs. Naomi J. Wilson, Columbus, O.; a brother, Norman B. Jennings, of Ventura; and seven grandchildren, Clarence Minnerly Jr., Santa Clara, James E. Minnerly, Ketchikan, Alaska, Sandra Lee Peto, N. Carlsbad, Elizabeth Ann Jennings, Visalia, Barbara Ann Peto, N. Carlsbad, Byron William Jennings III, Visalia, and Byron Jefferson Davis, Beaver Lodge, Alberta. He also is survived by two great grandchildren, Sydney A. and Robin Marie Minnerly, of Santa Clara.

Funeral services are to be held at the Hadley Chapel in Visalia Saturday at 11 a. m. The Rev. Victor M. Rivera will officiate, and the eulogy will be given by Superior Judge Wilko Machetanz.

Burial will be in the Deep Creek Cemetery, next to his wife, who died 42 years ago.

Friends have been requested by the family to contribute to the Tulare County Cancer Society instead of sending floral offerings.

Byron William Jennings Sr.
(1870 – 1955)

2

Byron William Jennings Jr.
(1911 – 1984)

My Father

Dick Crawford, Byron Jr., Byron Sr.

Byron Jr. was a *man's* man. He looked you straight in the eye. His handshake was firm. His word was his bond.

Wanda Walston and Byron, age 21

He was a *lady's* man. He was long, lean, and dapper. He knew how to dress and had an excess of charm. Girls swooned when they saw him coming. He swept them off their feet. He was a combination of John Wayne and Clark Gable, and he knew it. Byron's favorite saying was, "I can get more girlfriends on a horse than most guys can in a Cadillac."

Baby Byron

Byron William Jennings, Jr. was born in 1911, to Byron, Sr. and Elizabeth Ann, and was the only son with three older sisters. Another sister came two years later. Byron's mother, Lizzie, died when he was only two years old. Baby, Elizabeth, was just three months old. You will remember their mother died of a combination of pneumonia and a broken heart.

My Father

Thelma, Madge, Geri, three older sisters

Byron Jr. was raised by his father and three sisters. Since Grandpa never remarried, he hired an older couple to watch the kids. They went by Grandma and Grandpa Hummel, but they were not relatives. The Hummels were punitive and mean. Nobody told stories about them, and there is not even one photograph of them. It was not an easy upbringing. Byron's childhood was devoid of the nurturing of a mother's love. This lack haunted him all of his life. It colored his relationships with women and his self-assurance. The whole family was ruggedly independent and competitive.

Everyone had chores. Little Byron, as the smallest and youngest, usually got the hind-most. For example, the girls fed and watered the animals and Byron was left to shovel manure.

Farm boy, age 11   *Cowboy, age 9*

In the 1930s all the Jennings kids attended the original Deep Creek School, which was located across from Deep Creek Cemetery south of Effie Hillard's place on the highway and what is now called road 168.

Original Deep Creek School house

Original Deep Creek School
Byron 2nd row, 5th from left
Sisters, Madge & Geri on top row

Academics was not Byron's strong suit, yet he managed to get that high school diploma. He did have a fine reputation at the local pool hall, where he spent his lunch hours. Byron's Grandmother, Margaret Costly Jennings, lived out her days in Visalia, and Byron sometimes skipped the pool hall to check on her.

The summers at the coast were a relief from the heat of the San Joaquin Valley. Every June Byron Sr. sent the entire crew to the eucalyptus grove above Pismo Beach. As a young boy, Byron Jr. spent all summer in bare feet and raggedy cut-offs. The family camped, fished, went clamming, and played in the surf. Grandpa hired The Hummels to ride rough-shod over the kids, while he remained in the valley, harvesting and doing whatever else a man does when the kids are away.

My Dirty Dozen

Young Byron, like his father, soon learned his way around tractors, disks, orchards, field crops, and livestock, plenty of livestock. Their pride and joy was a stable of thoroughbred horses. They even built a dirt racetrack on the back of the property. It became well known and often used. Young Byron's job was gatekeeper. He let horses in one at a time, and caught a nickel or a dime when one was tossed his way.

Inheritor, 1940

IBN Grenada, polo stallion

Colt in front of Grandpa's barn

During the Depression, the sisters were sent away to private school, while Byron remained behind to help save the farm. As a young man, Byron worked at the home place and was leased out to work on the neighbors' farms. With the ingenuity of the old man, coupled with the hard work of the young, they managed to save the farm. Neighbors on all sides were going under.

Byron worshipped his father. He told of the comfort he felt when he wiped his face on his father's towel. The smell of the old man's sweat was sweet to him.

Byron's father was instrumental in organizing the Tulare County Mounted Sheriffs' Posse. Both father and son had gorgeous matching palominos and extravagant silver-mounted saddles and tack. They proudly rode in parades and horse shows and carried flags. They were quite the pair.

Members of Tulare County Mounted Sheriffs' Posse decked out

My Dirty Dozen

Byron Jr. and Mary Fisher got married in 1936 when they were twenty-five. They eloped because they were still terrified of their parents. They kept the pairing a secret for a good long while. Eventually they moved in together across the highway from the Old Man and checked on him every day until he died in 1955.

Byron and Mary

When asked if we were related to Peter Jennings, or better yet, Wayland Jennings, Bryon snickered and said, "Naw, the only Jennings that would ever claim us was Al Jennings, the Oklahoma bandit."

Al Jennings ran with the James boys

Beneath the humor, however, was a hint of inferiority. Byron and Mary hung out with the country club set, who were educated professionals. They collected sheepskins and law degrees, while Byron collected dust working eighteen hours a day for the neighbors and at home. Byron was a self-made man. He was proficient in cultivation, propagation, pollination, germination, transplantation, fertilization, irrigation, procreation, and conservation. He operated a corporation and was well informed about compensation as well as taxation. He was conversant on legislation and regulations. He was full of information and covered with perspiration.

During the war his friends served in uniform, while Byron grew food for the troops at home. He felt there was less honor farming than fighting in uniform. In spite of his many talents Bryon secretly believed he was inadequate deep down. He tried harder, worked longer, and laughed louder than his pals.

Many of those who could not join the military in WWII were recruited into the Aircraft Warning System, which was organized in 1941. At its peak there were 750,000 volunteers in the AWS, of which my parents were two. All volunteers received extensive training in aircraft recognition. When we heard the sound of an airplane, we ran out into the yard to identify it. I must have been two-and-a-half and didn't know what was going on. To me it was quite exciting. We heard a plane and everybody ran outside. Each aircraft was recorded in a log book and immediately called into the Army Filter Center. They called it a "flash message."

Examples of awards given AWS vonunteers

There were elaborate awards including certificates, arm bands, patches, and pins. NBC hosted a famous thirty-minute weekly radio broadcast called *Eyes Aloft*, with sixty-one episodes starring Henry Fonda. The Aircraft Warning System was disbanded in 1944, when I was three. Running out to look for airplanes looms large in my memory, in spite of the fact I was a little one.

My Father

Example of our old telephone

Late one night in 1947 the phone rang. (You know the old hardwood phones with the crank and ear piece on a wire.) I remember I was stunned to see my father throw on his pants over his pajamas – he was in such a hurry. *It was a fire! The stable! Oh no!* The stable was ablaze, but they never knew what started it. No fire truck came. (It would have been too late anyway.) Unbelievably, horses run into a fire by nature. All those beautiful thoroughbreds perished – all except one – Ginger. I can't imagine how devastated my dad and his father must have been. At least they saved the barn and the house.

My Dirty Dozen

Byron Sr.

Byron Jr. breaking a horse

Byron Sr. with show horse

Ginger was a pretty palomino, and she was smart, smart enough to kick her way out of that burning inferno and, against her nature, run *away* from the fire. Her left rump was badly burned, but she survived. After that we kept Ginger in our barn and doctored her wounds every day for years. She never totally recovered, but we loved her just the same.

Ginger, before the fire

Jennings Horses Take Fair Awards

B. W. Jennings and Son, Visalia rural district horse breeders, took honors last week with their Palaminos at the Tulare-Kings County fair in Tulare.

"Ginger," well-known to many who have attended rodeos in Visalia, took first prize in the stock horse class and third in the Palamino pleasure class. "Ginger" is six years old.

"Yellow Money" won first in his division in the breeding class. "Yellow Money" is a two-year-old.

"Ginger" won over horses exhibited from Long Beach, Pomona and Redwood City. B. W. Jennings, Sr., and his son, B. W. Jennings, Jr., exhibited four animals at the fair.

Byron made sure his family enjoyed varied cultural events. County fairs, horse shows, and rodeos were a given. But he didn't stop there. Every time a circus came to town, we were there in the front row. We had season tickets to the Civic Music Concert Series. The Ice Capades were a big hit. One time the international tennis stars at the time, Pancho Gonzales and Pancho Segura a gave an exhibition match in Visalia.

Pancho Segura

Pancho Gonzales

You know what stuck with me? Pancho Segura's legs were bowed from having had rickets as a child, yet he hit that double-handed forehand like a bullet. Let's not forget the time the Harlem Globe Trotters were in town. Their whistling and antics kept us in stiches and awe at the same time. It was also a tacit lesson in racism – an all black team in an all white town.

My Father

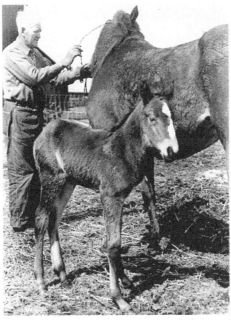

Gus (Augustus) Bequette in younger days helping with horses

When the holidays rolled around, our family piled in the car and paid a visit to a couple of elderly family friends. They were all alone, and we were their only visitors. One was Gus Bequette, a friend of Byron Sr. Gus was an interesting old coot, who lived into his nineties. My Grandfather told us that Gus's mother, as a child, was one of the few survivors of the Donnor Party. This was something we didn't discuss with Gus. We brought a box of oranges or a plate of cookies, and sat for a spell. It was completely silent, no TV, no radio, no nothing, and there was not a lot to discuss with an isolated old man. We went every year anyway, just to break up his boredom and spread a little light. It was yet another unspoken lesson in compassion and charity.

My Dirty Dozen

After Grandpa Fisher died my father realized his mother-in-law had no means of support. She had been a housewife all her life. Byron paid into social security the minimum quarters required to qualify his mother-in-law, for social security and health insurance. According to the internet her grant was sixty-two dollars a month as a widow. Had she been a man it would have been ninety-two dollars. But she lived and collected the pension for twenty-five years. My father had a soft heart. He wanted to help and he didn't need credit either. He never mentioned this charity. It was done on the hush-hush.

The big fisherman

It would not be a lie to call Byron "The Big Fisherman." He loved deep sea fishing. So when Murt Dula fired up his personal airplane and called, Byron was Johnny-on-the-spot.

My Father

Byron with Murt Dula and wife in Mexico

They typically spent a week or two in remote Baja, California. They smoked, drank, played cards, fished, and practiced bad Spanish with the locals. They came home with a pile of fish and many hard-to-believe stories. Byron entertained us with a drawn-out story about this Mexican woman, Margarita. She claimed the tequila and lime drink was named after her. Then there was the story of the one that got away – a sixty-pound albacore. That story made the newspaper. Byron was a great story-teller; nobody ever doubted him.

My parents' relationship heated up in the 1960s. His philandering grew, triggering Mother's paranoia. The mutual distrust came to a head. Hostility was rampant, and

My Dirty Dozen

tension was thick. I was nineteen and home from college. I tried my best to be a grown-up and be helpful. I figured it was my job to get them together. I built up Dad to Mother and extoled the virtues of Mother to Dad. It didn't work. I made things worse. I had failed to help and I felt crushed. I had to admit I was not an adult. I was defeated and sick to my stomach. This was our dark-cloud period. After twenty-eight years Byron and Mary divorced in 1962. The relationship was full of acrimony, and neither of them ever let go of the bitterness. They crossed the street to avoid one another.

After the separation, Byron lived in the country with a few of his cronies. They called it "The Bull Pen," because it was decorated with mounted heads of Texas longhorns, a place only a man could appreciate.

The Bullpen

My mother remained in the 2800 square-foot family home by herself.

Years later Byron Jr. parked his trailer at Pismo Coast Village and frequently returned to his old stomping grounds. He had fond memories of those summers he spent in Pismo as a kid, and it was a place of nostalgia for my Dad. In spite of his bravado, he was a sentimental guy.

Byron Jr. at Pismo Coast village circa 1980

Byron met Pamela Hessler, a younger English lady, in 1964 at a bar in Fresno. He turned on his charm, and she was a goner. One time he surprised her with a miniature poodle. That sealed the deal. They were married, and Pam became part of the family. But, alas, ten years later we endured yet another painful divorce. They went to court over the pots and pans.

My Dirty Dozen

Pamela, Byron, Mignon, the poodle, Pismo Beach

Yes, Byron was a man's-man and he was a lady's-man. He was a man who felt insecure on the inside, but you would never know it. He was too busy spinning yarns and entertaining anybody he could get to listen. Not unlike his father, he was well liked and well loved. He worked hard, and he played hard, and he lasted seventy-three years. He simply ran out of air.

Byron William Jennings Jr. 1911 – 1984

My Father

Byron Jennings

Tribute services will be at 7 p.m. Tuesday at the Visalia Elk's Lodge for Byron W. Jennings Jr., 73, a third-generation native of Visalia, who died Feb. 19 in Southern California.

Jennings had farmed east of Visalia for many years.

He married Mary Fisher in 1933 in Riverside. The couple lived in Visalia, where she died in 1983.

He was a member of Tehran Temple of the Scottish Rite, the Visalia Elk's Lodge, Visalia Moose Lodge, Visalia Country Club, Visalia Exchange Club and Tulare County Taxpayer's Association.

He was on the Tulare County Fair Board, the Tulare County Grand Jury, the Tulare County Farm Bureau, Cling Peach Advisory Board of Directors, Early California Apple Advisory Board, the California Citrus Mutual, Tulare County Rural Housing Board of Directors, Sequoia Walnut Growers Association, the Kaweah Delta Cooperative Cotton Gin, California Canners and Growers (a peach co-op), Tulare Growers Apple Co-op and served on various state advisory boards.

He is survived by one son, Byron W. Jennings III of Strathmore; one daughter, Anne Brazil of Visalia; three sisters, Thelma Sarrar of Honolulu, Hawaii, Geraldine Davis of Beaverlodge, Alberta, Canada, and Elizabeth Uhl of Pacific Grove; and one grandson.

Cremation was in Southern California.

Finale

Byron was adamant about having no funeral at all. We had a service at the Elks Club with an open bar. We put his ashes next to his parents in the Deep Creek Cemetery, a modest resting place. About a dozen neighbors were in attendance. We went against his wishes in a small way.

My brother and I arrived early with the ashes, to get things ready. We had no idea what we were doing, and we were in our dress-up clothes. We noticed a small piece of AstroTurf™ on the ground, and we bent over to investigate. There was a narrow, but deep, hole under that cover. The ashes were in a bronze box, not an urn. I was surprised at how heavy those ashes were. I placed the bronze box carefully on the AstroTurf™, and guess what! It fell into that deep hole! We were alarmed, to say the least. The people were driving up. Oh no! My brother got on his hands and knees in the dirt, in his nice clothes, and retrieved the box. We looked at each other and simultaneously burst out laughing at the sheer absurdity of the situation. I whispered ungently, "Hurry! Hurry! They're almost here." We knew our Dad was laughing right along with us. My brother retrieved that box in the nick of time, but his white shirt was ruined.

We proceeded with the brief service. Byron always said that family friend, Barbara Artis, had the voice of an angel. She agreed to sing *The Lord's Prayer*, unaccompanied. One or two neighbors related a fond memory. My brother and I tried valiantly not to look at each other so as not to break out in giggles again.

> Byron was put to rest in the same spirit as he lived, rising above the pain with a light heart.

Rest in Peace, Daddy

Byron William Jennings Jr.
(1911 – 1984)

My Dirty Dozen

3

Mary Wallace Fisher Jennings
(1911 – 1983)

My Mother

El Festino, ranch house in Lindsay provided for hired help

The Fisher household was thrilled when Mary Wallace Fisher, my mother, came into this world in 1911. Ben and Gertie, her parents, had been married five years and were ready for a child. They were proud as punch. She was their first, so naturally she was their best. Gertie kept her dressed nicely, and Ben made her behave.

My Dirty Dozen

Mary, age 3   Mary and Brother, Steve, on ranch

Mary was a clever girl. She thrived in school at the top of her class in most everything. She had her own opinions, but learned early on to keep them to herself. From her strict upbringing with no room for talking back or speaking up. She attended a country school, in Lindsay, California, Outside Creek.

Outside Creek School 1925

My Mother

Picture this: while mother, Mary Fisher, was attending Outside Creek School, my father attended Deep Creek School only ten miles through the fields. The country schools organized a concert to be held in Visalia at the Municipal Auditorium. Byron Jennings and the future Mrs. Byron Jennings were both in that concert. They knew each other back when they were ten, but they never dreamed what the future held in store for them.

My Dirty Dozen

Fisher Home on Exeter/Farmersville Blvd.

The Fishers moved from Lindsay to Exeter around 1925. They purchased a small grape ranch and house. Mary graduated from Exeter High School in 1928. She became a life member of the California Scholarship Federation and was awarded a stipend for college.

Mary 1927

My Mother

She was accepted into Pomona College, but there was no way she would be able to go. Unfortunately, the stipend was not enough. Ben and Gertie were not keen on education and had no intention of spending hard-earned money on something they considered so frivolous.

Mary was a determined youngster and immediately set out to get to college on her own. She saved up, got a job – and a great job it was. She and a friend waited tables at a resort in Lake Tahoe.

This was the life. Wait tables and collect tips at night, and play, play, play all day. Who could resist a face like that? Those tips got her to Pomona.

Mary Wallace Fisher
age 20 - circa 1931

My Dirty Dozen

Mary, 4th from left, with waitresses at Lake Tahoe

After two years Mary transferred to University of California at Berkeley. She received her degree in Costume Design in 1932. She was very handy with needle and thread and had a big dose of creativity. She was on the path to become another Edith Head, who was well known at the time for her design work in the movies.

But as fate would have it, she returned home and got a job in Visalia at The Model, a high-end dress shop. She lived at home in Exeter with her parents and saved her money. She must have enjoyed a healthy social life, judging from the pictures.

My Mother

Because they were born in the same year and lived in the same tiny community, Mary and Byron were bound to run into each other. I know only a few of the facts, so I will flesh out the rest of the story with my imagination. Byron was engaged to Wanda Walston. Wanda decided to marry Tom Crowe, the town lawyer. Tom is long gone and so is Wanda. In fact John and Danny Crowe, Tom's lawyer sons, are gone too. But I'm still alive and kicking, so you will have to take my word for it.

Back to Byron – What was a guy to do? Wanda was gone. Mary Fisher was easy on the eye, and she had a lot of class. They made a fine looking couple.

Mary and Byron became an item. At twenty-four they decided to get married, but there was *one* big problem. No, there were *two* big problems, his parents and her parents. Neither of them had a happy, secure childhood. Both Ben Fisher and Byron Jennings Sr. used fear as a method of parenting. Even at twenty-five, the couple was afraid to tell their parents about the pending marriage.

One weekend in the summer of 1936, on the spur of the moment, they jumped in the car and ran off to Riverside and got married. They lied on the marriage license saying that they were both from Palo Alto. I imagine they didn't want their parents to learn of the wedding in the *Visalia Times Delta*. They kept their secret for several long months and occasionally ducked out to a tiny apartment in Visalia to be together. Finally the cat was out of the bag, but it was too late for either family to stop them.

> **This Certifies**
>
> That on the *seventeenth* day of *July* in the year of our Lord *1936* *Byron William Jennings Jr.* from *Palo Alto* and *Mary Wallace Fisher* from *Palo Alto* were by me united in
>
> **Holy Matrimony**
>
> at *Riverside* According to the Ordinance of God and the laws of *California*
>
> Witnesses *Miriam W. Ellis*
>
> *Francis C. Ellis*
> Pastor

My Dirty Dozen

Family home across the highway from Grandpa

Mary, well put together while hanging wash

Mary and Byron moved to a modest ranch house across the highway from the home place and settled down to married life. Byron needed to be close-by in order to operate the farm with his father and keep an eye on Grandpa as he aged. Mary gave up her career to become Mrs. Byron Jennings Jr. and the mother of his children. There was never a question as to whether Mary would have a career other than being Byron's wife. No wife of his would ever work.

My Mother

Mary cooked three square meals a day; she canned, sewed, did laundry with a washboard and a clothesline. Getting that wringer washer was a big event in our household. Mary prided herself on her ability to cut corners and save by watching prices, making things by hand, and preparing delicious casseroles. Byron never shopped for himself. Mary dutifully brought home what she thought he needed to try and returned and exchanged what he rejected. Byron never saw the inside of a store (unless it was a hardware store.) My mother cheerfully fulfilled her duties as a wife and mother and looked good doing so. Mary was an educated and sophisticated woman. She strived to be the best wife she could be, and she subordinated her talents in favor of her husband's.

In five years little Anne was born, and after five more years Byron William Jennings III (Bill) came along. Mary was not a warm and fuzzy parent. Don't get me wrong, she did her job as wife and mother with precision. I never knew for sure she was listening to me. There was not a lot of eye contact. She didn't smile much. Sometimes she seemed to be in another world. As a little kid I didn't know what to expect. I didn't know what was normal. I didn't know anything was missing. I tried my best to stay out of the way, so as to avoid those cold, harsh reprimands. Aside from the time spent with my father, I learned to amuse myself. I played in the dirt, picked wildflowers, and rescued dogs and cats.

The mother little Anne remembers

Mother with Anne and Bill

The Jennings Family - Circa 1948
Byron III (Bill) - Mary - Byron Jr - Anne

My Mother

On the other hand there were the memorable moments. Some might be called endearing. The next chapter, *So So Sewing,* is one such experience.

We made apple sauce and canned peaches in the summer. It was unbearbly hot, but even so, Grandma was there, and that always made me happy. My mother did not want to displease her mother, so she was easy on me when Grandma was there. The atmosphere was always calmer when we had company. We sat at the kitchen table and peeled and sliced and sweltered. We canned enough fruit to last through the winter. There was no need to shop for produce. We made the most amazing applesauce and pies from the fruit picked fresh off our trees. White Astrachan apples were cooking apples. They were green and crisp and very tart. Taking a bite out of a fresh Astrachan apple was not for the faint of heart. The flavor however was unbeatable. As a youngster I sat under a tree at the side of the highway, and sold bushel boxes of culls for a dollar. Sadly new White Astrachan apple trees were not planted, and once the old trees died, that was the end. That also, ended my affair with apple sauce and apple pies. Todays fruit simply doesn't have that White Astrachan zing.

My Dirty Dozen

In addition to canning, mother made sure we had special meals. I remember the hearty breakfasts of two eggs, basted, two slices of bacon, crisp, and a little bowl with a perfect half of a canned peach in heavy syrup. Thanksgiving and Christmas dinners were exquisite. Easter was huge with colored eggs and a big meal. Her birthday was Columbus Day, so that was always special. There was Fourth of July with red, white, and blue food. On Valentine's Day she put a little favor under every plate. There was St. Patrick's Day with a green cake. There were birthdays in February and October. My mother did it all, year after year after year. She never asked for help, and she acted as if it was her greatest pleasure.

How could I forget one April Fool's Day. It fell on a Sunday. She made home-made biscuits from scratch. I can smell them right now, just as they were when she delivered a big tray of steaming hot biscuits with gobs of melting butter. Our mouths watered as we took that first bite. Guess what! Something was stringy and white. Eeew, what was it? My mother had put cotton in each biscuit. *April Fool!* That was so out of character for Mother. We were the pranksters; she was the serious one. We laughed till we cried. She *got* us good. But she made sure there was a backup batch of good biscuits waiting in the wings.

Another childhood memory had to do with grocery shopping. During the war many items were rationed. When in the check-out line, Mother carried the ration book, and I got to hold the tokens that were used for change. I took my job seriously and gripped those tiny wooden discs for dear life.

My Mother

Ration book　　　　Ration Pouch　　　　Ration tokens

Speaking of food, my Mother suffered from severe food allergies. Most fruits and many nuts sent her into, what we now term as anaphylactic shock. In those days we knew only that if she had a attack, she had to be rushed to a hospital for a massive shot of adrenaline. While this condition was life-threatening, Mother never let it stand in her way. Mother cheerfully dashed five miles into Visalia, with Bill's Little League and football games, my music concerts, and all that comes with raising active kids. She continued to play in golf tournaments, enjoy Tuesday Luncheon Bridge, and American Association of University Woman, (AAUW).

Mary, on right, at the country club

Balancing family, health, and social responsibilities must have been a strain, but Mary appeared, at least on the outside, to handle everything without complaint. I remember that she always answered the phone with a musical "Hello," no matter what yelling match was going on at the time.

Her outlook, as to her place as a mother, was remarkable. One time Mary was at her bridge club, and one of the ladies said something like this: "Isn't Anne lucky to have travelled all over the world." This infuriated my mother. She argued, "Luck had nothing whatever to do with it. Anne has earned everything she gets in life. She is industrious and capable, and smart. Not lucky." My mother aligned herself with the words of Kahil Gibran.

Your children are not your children.
They are the sons and daughters of Life's longing for itself.
They come through you but not from you,
And though they are with you yet they belong not to you.

My Mother

Mary had kept up her end of the bargain, but was her husband doing his part? She could no longer ignore his flirtations with other women. She wondered what was going on behind her back. Byron was always gone to one Farmer's Board meeting or another. Then he started to spend more and more time at the country club. He couldn't have played golf at three in the morning. He drank, played cards, and gambled till all hours in order to hide from building tensions at home. Byron became increasingly distant. He felt completely justified in his actions, and became indignant by her allegations. Mary could not reconcile his inconsistencies. Soon the sacrifices she had made all those years became meaningless. The countless incongruities were tearing Mother apart.

Mary's intuition kicked in, and she began keeping journals. She documented Byron's comings and goings by date and time, and began to find patterns in these activities. Mary believed that Byron wanted her out of the way, so he could pursue his promiscuity without interference. Our family had always been loud, but this was a notch above. She accused. He defended. They yelled. She protested. He escalated. Byron was a big man, and usually won by virtue of his size, but when that failed, he overpowered with ruthless, hurtful names and a thundering voice. He got loud and he got mean. We all feared my father's rage. It might have turned physical, but it rarely did. The worry was always there. The fighting was frequent, and, in the end, they retreated to their respective corners, seething and covering it with alcohol.

Bill and I steered clear. He was in high school and disappeared with his friends. I was on summer break from San Jose State and thought it was my job to get them back together. I parked myself on Mother's sofa, knitted and watched TV. When Dad was gone, I tried to reason with Mother. When Dad came in, I tried to talk sense into him. Of course my efforts were futile. In the end I felt insignificant and sick to my stomach.

It was the 1950s, before women's lib, and men still had all the power. The constant arguments with Mary became unbearable to Byron, and he decided to *do* something. One day he ushered us kids out of the house. He called in Mary's brother, Steve, and the family doctor, Dr. Twinem. The three men in her life issued an ultimatum to Mary. (This would have been termed an intervention had it occurred today.) They told her that she was irrational and needed to go to the hospital. They told her she had no choice. She could go willingly, or they would declare her mentally incompetent, and they would take her forcibly.

Bill and I were not there. Our father told us later that she decided to go willingly to Kings View Mental Hospital in Reedly, CA. It was a nice facility offering the latest and greatest of care. I remember that Mother described a different senario. In her writings, she alleged that she was taken "kicking and screaming," and she was drugged and put in a padded room for a week. Who knows what the truth is, but either way, it was a devastating coup. Every man Mary loved and trusted had turned against her. She never really recovered from that betrayal.

My Mother

Mary entered the hospital as a patient in 1960. It was several weeks before she was allowed visitors. I remember walking into that institution with much trepidation. I never knew my Mother was crazy. I didn't know what to expect. I was afraid. I was confused. My stomach churned. I perspired. I wanted to be supportive, but I didn't know how. I was surprised that she seemed pretty normal. She was maybe a little too bright-eyed and bushy-tailed, but relatively close to the same old mother I knew.

I was shocked to see Mary's name at the top of every activity list. My mother refused to participate in such messy, icky, yucky actvities with the family. We could never get her to ride a horse, swim in the irrigation ditch, or ride an innertube down the St. John's River. Nosiree! She was the clean and pressed type. She preferred the more cultured, formal side of life. But there it was, Mary's name on every list for bowling, picnics, and bike rides. She even made those atrocious mosiac ashtrays. She would have played Tiddlywinks had they offered it.

Remember our determined young girl? At the hospital Mary put that quality to work immediately. She out-foxed her psychiatrist. Mary was one sharp cookie. She had a minor in psychology, and she outsmarted the system. She played the game, and she played it well, and got herself out of that place in ten weeks. Mary never recovered from the humiliation of that experience, or from forever being labeled a paranoid schizophrenic. She certainly never forgave Byron, or her brother, or Dr. Twinem.

My Dirty Dozen

How did the community react to our family's misfortune? Did anyone come to the door with a casserole? No! Did anybody send a card of encouragent? No! Did anyone offer to help in any way at all? No! Once in a while the doorbell rang. My brother or I answered, and we were asked in a whiny-sarcastic tone, "Is your Mother home? Where is she?" People were not kind. People wanted a reason to gossip. There was overwhelming ignorance and lack of acceptance of mental illness in those days. There was no support whatsoever. We were on our own.

While Mary was away, Byron had free rein to conceal as many assets as possible, in case of a divorce. After her hospitalization things were never the same at home. The tension was thick. After twenty-eight years Byron and Mary parted ways. Mary was outraged when Byron expected her to accept what he thought was good for her in the settlement. She got her own lawyer and fought him with all her might. He took this as a challenge and fought back even harder. Everything was fair game. He wanted to keep the ranch intact. She wanted her fair share. In the end Mary got a portion of the orange grove in Strathmore, a portion of the homeplace in Farmersville, and the house. It cost her dearly, but she dug her heels in and held her ground. Years later in an effort to restore the orange grove, Byron managed to purchase Mary's portion through a third party without her knowledge. That clearly spoke to Byron's usual dirty tricks.

Mary always suspected Byron had hidden assets somewhere, and she investigated persistently. This only served to confirm Byron's claim that she was crazy. What a crushing double bind. It outweighed the hundreds of double binds she endured in the marriage. She was outraged. She was hurt. She was devastated. She was never the same after the divorce. It was too much to bear. And yes, they crossed the street to avoid one another.

Mary's house 2015

Mary was a proud woman and was able to keep up appearances. She hung in there with two bridge clubs, and still answered the phone with that musical voice. Otherwise she retreated within herself. I can still picture my mother in that big house doing the few things she had left to do: sitting at her kitchen table, working crossword puzzles, watching Perry Mason, smoking Parliaments, and drinking vodka.

My Dirty Dozen

Mary, near the end

My mother, Mary, fought the good fight. She lost. She was ahead of her time. Had she lived today, she would have had a fighting chance. Back then she was all alone, and she had no chance at all.

My brother found her in her bed. Her heart had stopped.
Of course it did!
It was broken!

Rest in Peace, Mother, in that place where there is only perfect love.

My Mother

Mary Wallace Fisher Jennings
(1911 – 1983)

My Dirty Dozen

4
So So Sewing

Having spent my early years outdoors with animals and trees, riding horses, and tractors, and playing in barns, 4-H Club seemed like a natural progression. I was in my ninth year when I walked into that first club meeting with a feeling of excitement and dread. I didn't know what to expect. Seeing the novice leaders stand before the entire group conducting a meeting struck terror in my heart. If that was what I had to look forward to, count me out. My primary objective was to remain invisible and not get called on. At the end of the meeting it was time to sign up for a project. There were chickens and horses and goats, oh my! What was new and interesting about that? Cooking and sewing would have to do. The cooking part has faded from memory, (maybe I didn't like the food,) but sewing took hold.

First project – a scarf. Cut fabric and hem it by hand. Mine was lopsided, but at least there were no blood stains from those lethal pins and needles.

Second project – a blouse, a cap-sleeved blouse. That required a tissue paper pattern. My dear mother patiently demonstrated how to open and unfold the fragile pattern. We spread the flour sack print cloth on the dining room table. It was a challenge for a nine year old to stick a pin through that tissue and the fabric and back up without tearing the pattern or mussing the cloth. Mother, having studied costume design, punched through and was finished in half a second. She couldn't understand how anyone could make such a mess of it. She lovingly demonstrated anyway but ended up doing most of it herself.

Now it was time to cut. Which line? Should we select the dotted line or the solid? Mother let me use her prized shears that were always hidden away so as to never be ruined by cutting paper or chicken bones or anything but fabric. I was a big girl now. I maneuvered around curves and seam allowances, darts and everything grown up. Those unwieldy shiny scissors hurt my hand, but I never let on. I didn't want to waste my good fortune.

Mother held a small supply of pins between her teeth, but she warned me to never ever do that. To this day I still commit the unforgivable sin of holding a few pins between my lips. It is handy and my mother did it. She showed me how to make a little slash in the seam allowance where the notch should be, and how to pin seams rather than baste. She taught me all her secret shortcuts.

The sewing machine was stored in the corner of my bedroom under the window to the porch. Since the laundry room was really an enclosed back porch, that window opened onto the laundry. While Mother folded clothes, I sewed. After every seam I took the garment to her, to set up the next seam. I couldn't read the pattern instruction sheet. My mother, who could have zipped out that blouse in an hour, took all day to guide me step by step. Finally I was able to claim I made my first cap-sleeved blouse. I showed it at the Tulare County Fair. I won a blue ribbon, too. Everyone said Helen Moos, the 4-H leader, taught me to sew. It was really my mother, who was there every step of the way. She gave me the gift of sewing.

I graduated to a set-in-sleeve blouse and many other creations. We spent hours in the fabric store. We selected just the right pattern, and picked out the perfect fabric. Mother was drawn to an olive drab, mustard, and neutral color scheme. I, on the other hand, loved the bright, clear tones. I teased Mother about her selections, and she gave me a hard time about mine. She never stated out loud that she thought my fabric was gaudy and garish, but I knew what she was thinking. I thought her choices were atrocious. Even now you won't catch me wearing green. Instead, I think of mother and smile every time I see that muddy green color. I learned how to visualize a garment pictured in one fabric but made up in another. This became a useful skill which I still use in my art, home decorating, and even gardening.

Lanz dresses and Capezio shoes were popular with the in-crowd in 1958. A Lanz dress, at that time, ran about fifty dollars. That was out of the question for us. You may remember those dresses were made of high quality cotton with a tiny print on white or pastel. They were trimmed with rickrack around the neckline and hem. Mother and I found a Lanz-like print at the store one day. We had lots of rickrack at home. I made my own Lanz knock-off. It had a fitted bodice with a very full skirt and lots of crinolines. I found a pair of ballet slippers to imitate Capezios, and I was half-way to the in-crowd.

My Dirty Dozen

All the senior girls purchased prom dresses. I had a date; all I needed was a dress. We found a lovely white eyelet at the store. I lined the bodice with bright red percale. I made yards and yards of bias ribbon from the remnants, which I threaded in and out of the eyelet holes of the skirt. It was an advanced project, but with mom's assistance, I pulled it off. I had matching red pumps too.

Eyelet prom dress

Lanz knock-off

By this time I was on my own with my sewing. She claimed I had passed her up – that I was a better seamstress than she – but I didn't believe it. She gave the gift of sewing to me along with a lot of love. It became a cherished collaboration for us both.

My Dirty Dozen

5

Elizabeth Aileen Jennings Ball Uhl
(1913 – 1990)

Aunt Liz

It was February 6, 1913, when Elizabeth Jennings was born to Byron and Lizzie. It so happened, that Ronald Reagan also came into this world on that exact day and year. As a staunch Democrat, it always irked Elizabeth that she and Reagan shared a birthday.

Our family seems to have a tradition of honoring our ancestors. Her mother was Elizabeth Ann. I am Elizabeth Anne. My father's youngest sister, and the subject of this chapter, was Elizabeth. And then there is cousin Barbara Ann, and her daughter, Anne Elizabeth. You would think there was a shortage of names, there are so many Williams, Annes, Byrons and Elizabeths. Instead this custom gives me a feeling of royalty.

But on with her story.... Elizabeth was only three months old when her mother, Lizzie Jennings, died. Because she was such a tiny baby, it would have been impossible for Grandpa Jennings to take proper care of an infant as well as his four other children. Elizabeth was informally adopted by Jackson and Nellie Ball who were friends but unrelated. It is curious as to why kinfolk, Jennings or Davis, who lived in the area didn't step up to help Byron Sr., suddenly widowed and left with five kids. Grandpa certainly had his hands full. Was there bad blood between the relatives? We can only wonder. In any case Elizabeth was always considered to be a member of both the Ball and the Jennings families.

Elizabeth Jennings Ball about age 3

Regrettably, Elizabeth was a lonely little girl. She went to grammar school in Visalia from 1919 to 1927. Since her adopted parents, the Balls, were well-to-do she was escorted to school in a limousine by a chauffeur. She never got to walk to school and make friends like most kids. The family also employed Emma Nelson, a maid, who tended to Elizabeth's every need. I bet Emma occasionally slipped Elizabeth cupcakes on the side. Jackson Ball, her father, died when Elizabeth was twelve, leaving her alone with her mother and a much older brother, Harvey, and two servants. She tended to cover up her feelings of isolation by eating.

Elizabeth attended Dominican High School in San Rafael, California, from 1928 to 1932 with her biological sisters Geraldine and Marge Jennings. It was a private Catholic school run by the Sinsinawa Dominican nuns.

Dominican High School, San Rafael, California

After high school Elizabeth enrolled in Occidental College, a highly regarded private liberal arts school located in Los Angeles.

Occidental College in 1920s

Elizabeth purchased a lovely home at 500 N. Court Street in Visalia at some point prior to 1934. I remember the two huge white columns at the entry and luxury inside and out. Kenneth Kimura and his wife, Kiyo, and two small children, Kiyogo and Shachiko, lived in the servant's quarters in the rear.

Elizabeth sailed to Hawaii with her Mother, Nellie, and stepbrother Harvey Gilmore in 1934. They boarded the luxury liner, SS Malolo, on August 3rd and arrived in Honolulu on August 9th. I don't know how long they stayed in Hawaii, but she would have had to be back in time for school in the fall.

Aunt Liz

On the way to Hawaii, 1934

Elizabeth did not interrupt her education, while acquiring her own home and sailing to Hawaii. She transferred from Occidental to Stanford, in Palo Alto, California where she received her degree in Home Economics in 1936.

Stanford Church

After college Elizabeth and her mother sailed to New York to celebrate her college degree. They voyaged through the Panama Canal on the passenger liner, the SS Santa Rosa.

Passenger liner, SS Santa Rosa

Elizabeth enjoyed a prestigious education, yet she refused to talk about it. She believed doing so would seem pretentious. She took advantage of her education, however, by teaching Home Economics at Visalia High School for a few years.

Elizabeth met John Phelan in Visalia when she was twenty-six. Soon they were married, and all seemed well. John was a soft-spoken gentle man who had studied to be a priest for years. Once he was married, he began to wonder if he had made the right decision. He was torn between marriage and life as a priest. Even though Elizabeth understood and was supportive of John, that wasn't enough. He was ripped apart by this horrible dilemma. John committed suicide after nine months of marriage. Elizabeth was devastated. She wondered what she did wrong.

The next year Elizabeth married Kenneth Uhl, but after another nine months Ken tragically passed. Ken was a hemophiliac, and he accidentally cut himself in the shower. By the time Elizabeth arrived to help, it was too late; he bled to death.

Elizabeth suffered another setback in 1942 during World War II. The beloved Japanese family, the Kimuras, who helped raise her, was sent away to the Japanese internment camp in Arizona. They were stripped of all their land and possessions and incarcerated. These people were friends; they were family; they were not the enemy. It was not until 1945 that the Kimuras were released. They returned home to Visalia penniless. Elizabeth immediately gave them a small place to live and employment. It was a sad time.

Elizabeth was always a generous soul. She had a tendency to shower her suitors with lavish gifts. Her good intentions may have driven potential beaus away. She wondered if she was the bringer of bad luck. Elizabeth never remarried, but she shared her life with Victor Unger until his death in the 1983. Vic and Elizabeth enjoyed common interests. They liked learning about and collecting antiques. Vic was always surprising Elizabeth with some exquisite trinket. Vic was considered part of our family. I loved him like an uncle. While the relationship appeared to be romantic, many years later Aunt Liz shared with me that it was platonic, but with a depth of loving friendship that lasted forty years.

Elizabeth was the original feminist. While most women were in the kitchen baking, Elizabeth operated a business, bought property, managed picking and packing crews against the tide of the 40s and 50s. As a young girl I watched her round up a row of tin shacks for migrant workers to live in while they worked her walnut groves.

My Dirty Dozen

*Tin shacks on the way to Linnel Camp for migrant workers
Elizabeth's brother, Byron Jr., on right*

Elizabeth was able to run a business and manage people above and beyond what was considered normal for a woman at the time. She always maintained her femininity while she upheld straight forward dealings with men. She made sure her farm workers had housing and were not living in tents. Not only did she manage her farming operation, she was also the landlord of the Sequoia Auto Theater in the 1950s. My friends and I made liberal use of that drive-in theater when we were teenagers.

Sign on highway 198 and road 156

Aunt Liz

The entire family was considered to be big-boned. Aunt Liz, true to her heritage, grew up to be six feet and at least two hundred pounds depending on the current diet and proximity to the holidays. She was a classy dresser. She presented that big frame with dignity and style and spared no expense in doing so.

Elizabeth in her condo in Carmel

Her personality was larger than life, too. She never withheld her opinions, which were big-hearted but firm, nevertheless. People may have talked about Elizabeth's eccentricities, but she was not deterred by naysayers. She was self-assured and intent on getting the job done. She had no time for gossip. She was goal-oriented and successful in spite of raised eyebrows.

My Dirty Dozen

When Elizabeth was in her forties, in 1953, cancer of the bladder reared its ugly head. By the time the doctors discovered the problem, it was too late to operate, so radiation, though imprecise, was the only option in those days. She endured several rounds of radiation, and most of them were quite painful. It turned out the doctors had poisoned her body. The radiation had actually burned her internal organs. She landed back in the hospital, and things were touch-and-go.

In later years during a private moment Aunt Liz shared with me a mystical experience. She was lying in the hospital room all alone, and a spirit appeared at the foot of her bed. She could not be sure who it was, but she felt reassured and loved and was not alarmed whatsoever. Suddenly, what felt like a bolt of lightning coursed through her body. Something had happened, and it was big. After the spirit disappeared she had a feeling of wholeness and contentment. She knew she had a purpose to live and plenty of time to complete that purpose. The burns healed and the cancer never returned. Aunt Liz carried on another thirty-five years spreading her personalized version of love wherever she went. I was lucky enough to get my fair share. I remember after the death of my father she supported me when I most needed a friend.

Aunt Liz and her companion, Victor Unger, decided to get away from the hot summers and foggy winters of Visalia, and retired to the cool climate of the California coast in 1963. They lived on the 17-Mile Drive at the edge of the famous Pebble Beach Golf Course until his death in 1983.

View from 17 mile drive in Pebble Beach, California

Soon after, Aunt Liz relocated to nearby Pacific Grove. She enjoyed a few years there before she retired to Del Mesa Carmel, a gated community that provided all levels of assistance from independent living to dining room, nursing services, and memory care.

My Dirty Dozen

Inside her Carmel condo with Chinsee her prized Shar Pei

Elizabeth's outgoing personality, upbringing, and old money allowed her to hob-nob with celebrities living in Carmel. She used to lunch with Clint Eastwood's mother.

Clint Eastwood's mother, Ruth 1909-2006

She also claimed to know William Randolph Hearst and his paramour, Marion Davies.

Even though she had no children of her own, she influenced the lives of a number of her nieces and nephews. When her sister, Thelma, decided to move to Alaska, Elizabeth agreed to take in Thelma's two sons, Clarence and Corky. She raised and educated them, brought them up to speed on social graces, and instilled the drive for accomplishement. Clarence grew up to be quite successful in real estate development and farming. But when he wanted to marry Ann Torres, a wonderful Spanish girl, Elizabeth opposed the union. Being strong-willed like the rest of the family, Clarence married Ann anyway. Sadly, the relationship between Clarence and Elizabeth, his second mother, became distant.

Clarence Minnerly and wife, Ann Torres Minnerly

I visited Aunt Liz from time to time when she lived in Carmel and I lived in Visalia, and later Los Osos, California. She always made my visits an event. Often she took me for a luscious halibut dinner at a high-end bistro, and sometimes we purchased several pounds of fresh crab legs. We brought them home and feasted on lettuce and lemon and crab till juice ran down our elbows. She wanted me to dress with sophistication and took me to an upscale boutique. She was intent on dressing me properly.

Elizabeth was a spiritual woman. She quietly studied the writings of Joseph Campbell, a metaphysical philosopher and writer.

Joseph Campbell circa 1984

Campbell travelled widely, studied deeply, and subscribed to the teachings of Carl Jung. He discovered commonalities among cultures of the world. He wrote *The Power of Myth* and *The Hero's Journey* and originated the phrase "Follow your bliss." Aunt Liz and I connected on a spiritual level and enjoyed hours of metaphysical and mystical discussions. We decided we were spiritual sisters. She was more than an aunt to me. She was a role model, a teacher, friend, confidant, and soul sister.

When Aunt Liz passed, I was forty-nine. I remember it was November of 1990. As soon as I heard, I rushed to Carmel from Los Osos in the pouring rain to arrange a small memorial service for a few of her friends. I was touched that Clarence, her estranged nephew, flew in from Santa Barbara to attend in spite of his previous rift with Aunt Liz. He also insisted on picking up the tab for the flowers, the food, the facility, and the harpist.

As for her will she left her BMW and most of her sizable estate and belongings to her long time caretaker and maid, Mary Lou Harlan. She was more than a maid. Yes, Mary Lou called her Mrs. Uhl, but there was a warmth and devotion between the two. This decision had certain logic to it, as Mary Lou was there for her when she needed her, up to the very end.

MaryLou Harlan, the maid.

Two years after her death Aunt Liz came to me in spirit in March of 1992. I was meditating and became aware of her presence. In thought I stood and reached up for a hug. I knew it really was my Auntie Liz. She was tall. I could hear the rattle of her beads. I could smell her sweet perfume. I could feel her familiar arms around me. I remember telling her in thought. "You must be busy on the other side. You don't need to take time out to come see me." She said "I do need to come. I need to tell you how proud I am of you. You are doing the right thing. You are doing a good job."

Now I ask you, isn't that what we all want to hear?

Elizabeth Uhl

Elizabeth Aileen Ball Uhl, a walnut rancher and teacher, died Friday at Community Hospital of the Monterey Peninsula. She was 77. NOV 27 1990

Born in Visalia on Feb. 6, 1913, Mrs. Uhl was a walnut rancher in Visalia before moving to Carmel in 1963. She also taught at Visalia High School.

She is survived by a sister, Thelma Farrar of Hawaii, and seven nieces and nephews.

Private memorial services have been held. The California Cremation Society was in charge of the arrangements and ashes will be scattered at sea.

The family suggests that any memorial contributions be sent to the donor's favorite charity.

Elizabeth Aileen Jennings Ball Uhl
(1913 – 1990)

6

Marjorie Elizabeth Jennings Peto
(1906 – 1976)

Auntie Marge

I heard the grown-ups call her *Madge*, but none of us kids were allowed to use it. "It's Auntie *Marge*," they told us firmly. She hated that name *Madge*, hated it! I figured it had something to do with coming of age, and leaving the things of youth behind. She was the second child born to Byron and Lizzy Jennings, and yes she was a farm girl.

Thelma and Madge, 1909

Thelma, Geri, Madge, front porch

Original Deep Creek School – Madge top row, 2nd from right

All the Jennings kids went to the neighborhood school, Deep Creek. It was good preparation. Their father supplemented book learning by teaching his children proper attire, manners, and conduct in all social settings.

Schoolgirl Marge   *Marge, age 25*

Along with her sisters Marge attended Dominican High School. She enrolled at Fresno State College in 1925. While she was away at school, she decided to cut her hair, which was most likely an act of rebellion. Her father did not approve. He flew into a rage and beat her up, so the story went. Her father cut off the money. After only two years Marge quit school to spite her father. She moved to Long Beach, California, in short order, where she boarded with family friends, the Crawfords. Right away she got a job selling dry goods (textiles, ready-to-wear clothing, and sundries). Later she secured a position with the *Press Telegram* newspaper as a reporter. She saved until she secured her own place in Long Beach on 269 Quincy Ave.

Auntie Marge

269 Quincy Ave, Long Beach, California

Marge was a busy girl what with working and setting up her home. There was no doubt she enjoyed an active social life. Records show she took a ship to Hawaii in 1934. I imagine this was a family vacation. Maybe her father cooled down after the hair debacle.

After several years of living the good life she met Fax Peto on a blind date, a dapper gent from British Columbia. He was handsome, charming, and he took her dancing. They seemed to hit it off and soon became a couple. They wasted no time getting married in 1936. The following year Fax became a United States citizen. This was a huge event in his life and he talked about it with pride.

Fairfax Grant Peto   *Fax and Marge*

My Dirty Dozen

Sandra Lee came along in 1938 and the next year Marge gave birth to twin girls. They did not survive. The loss of those babies was a terrible tragedy and setback to Marge and the family. But Barbara Ann made her appearance on December 7, 1941. When Marge came out of anesthesia, the Japanese had bombed Pearl Harbor.

This period of adversity took its toll on Auntie Marge. The doctors discovered a lump in her breast. It was malignant, and she had a mastectomy soon thereafter. Aunt Elizabeth, the youngest of the Jennings clan, moved in with the Peto family to help care for her two nieces and her sister, Marge, while she recovered. They didn't know how long Marge would survive after cancer, so they took another trip to Hawaii. This time it was their father, Byron Sr., and sisters, Elizabeth and Marge, who set sail.

Once they realized she was going to live, they breathed a sigh of relief. Auntie Marge had had a single mastectomy and wore a prosthesis. I guess it was not that comfortable or well-fitted, as she appeared lopsided most of the time. It didn't bother me. That was just Auntie Marge, and I loved her the way she was. The whole family was secretive and hush-hush about it. There was the occasional whisper, making it clear that we were not to let on we knew anything. I went along with the charade, though I didn't understand why. My younger cousin, Barbara, later shared with me a story about her family. When they were home alone, Marge removed her prosthesis and tossed it on a chair. If the doorbell rang, they scurried around and tossed a pillow over it and acted as if nothing were there.

Fax was a travelling salesman with the United States Army Ordnance. He distributed arms to the U S Army troops. During the war he must have been transferred to San Francisco, as I remember when the Petos lived in a Victorian row house there. I have a vivid image of the house in my mind. As a farm girl used to the open spaces, it was really spooky to drive into a tiny underground, single-car garage. Inside, the house was cramped yet neat, and the small rooms were crowded with lots of formal furniture and knick-knacks everywhere. I was afraid I would break something. In spite of this it was always fun to visit Auntie Marge, Uncle Fax, and the girls.

Example of Victorian Row Houses

Uncle Fax lived up to his rather stuffy name, Fairfax Peto. He was a stiff-upper-lip kind of guy, who wore a smoking jacket to the dinner table and insisted on a formal linens, silverware, and crystal. If the children accidentally giggled at the table, they were promptly excused. Every morning he ate a soft boiled egg from an egg cup. I watched in disgust as he relished the process. First he carefully tapped around the top of the egg with a knife and removed the small disk of shell and morsel of egg white that he savored. I paid close attention as I soon had to follow suit. Next he scooped the runny egg out of the shell with that tiny spoon and picked up a triangle of toast to dip into the barely cooked egg. I didn't want this, but that was breakfast, and there was nothing else. I had to behave, or I would be excused. I wanted to be a good girl, so I ate the yucky egg anyway. I will never forget Uncle Fax and his egg cup.

After the war there was not much need for munitions and thus no need for Army Ordnance. Fax lost his job, returned to Montrose, California, and rented a house from his brother, Guy Peto. Guy was an attorney for the ACLU and his wife was a card-carrying communist. Barbara Ann remembers her sister, Sandra Lee, coming home with her front teeth knocked out. Someone beat her up because her aunt was a communist.

We three cousins had a lot of fun together through the years. Sandra Lee was two years older than I, and Barbara Ann a year younger. When they visited the farm we rode horses and swam in the irrigation ditch. When I stayed with them, we played cards, watched TV, and ate out. We were the proverbial city and country mice.

Anne, Barby, Sandy on May, the palomino

I always looked up to Sandra Lee and tried, not very successfully, to emulate her. She was advanced, intellectually, socially and developmentally, if you know what I mean. Barbara Ann was an easy-going, dreamy sort of kid, always happy to be last out of the gate. She got saddled with the nickname, *the cow's tail*. To this day Barby despises that term, while I still giggle.

During these years Uncle Fax found a job selling cars for DW Denham Ford dealership in Los Angeles. He was quite successful as a salesman and worked his way up to general manager. The family relocated after only two years to Montrose, California, on Sierra Vista Drive. This house was in a nice neighborhood with curbs, gutters and beautiful gardens.

Once when I stayed in Montrose, I went outside on a summer morning to visit with the neighbor over the back fence. His name was Clarence Nash. They called him "Ducky" because he was the voice for Donald Duck. He talked to us in Donald Duck's voice. I was star-struck. I was oh-so-curious, and yet tongue tied. It was hard to wrap my mind around someone famous being just a normal next-door neighbor. I peered through the curtains from time to time trying to get another glimpse of "Ducky." The Petos had a television. It was a thirteen-inch black and white console. We had no such luxury. I was in love. I got up early to sneak down and watch Roy Rogers and Hop-a-Long-Cassidy before Auntie Marge made me go play with the other kids. Even today television feels extravagant to me.

My Dirty Dozen

Another special memory was when Auntie Marge set up the picnic table and benches on the back porch. She brought us a red checkered oil cloth so we could play cards. We played hours and hours of Canasta.

The first Bob's Big boy in Glendale, California

When we got hungry, Auntie Marge piled us girls in the car. We got to have the biggest, juiciest hamburgers in the world at Bob's Big Boy. Once in a while she cooked, but I think having company gave Auntie Marge an excuse to go out to eat. I spent a month or more every summer with the Petos. Auntie Marge provided a warm and nurturing environment in those years, compared to the cooler and stricter atmosphere of home. I never got homesick, not *ever*.

The Petos moved again in the late 40's to a nice place in Glendale. It was a one-hour commute each way for Uncle Fax to WD Denham in Los Angeles. Finally Fax had the opportunity to join his brothers, Guy and Eric, in a large Ford dealership in Orange County, California. It was called Peto Motors and included a store in Escondido, one in Vista, and one in Oceanside.

Fire Mountain Drive, Oceanside, California

So the Petos relocated to Oceanside, California, up on Fire Mountain Drive. To my country eyes this home was spectacular, with views that went forever. Summers there still included Canasta, but by then we girls were teenagers. There I learned about *True Romance* magazines and talking on the phone for hours. Once Auntie Marge told Sandra Lee to get off the phone, but Sandy ignored her. Auntie Marge was having a little drinky-poo, as the whole family usually did. Soon the argument escalated and, out of character, Auntie Marge marched into the hall and yanked that phone jack right out of the wall. I was shocked but kept my mouth shut.

A typical scene was the men in the living room visiting and having a martini, while the women stayed in the kitchen. Auntie Marge rattled and banged the pots and pans, so the men thought she was cooking, and then she brought out a tray of crackers and cheese. Dinner was served at maybe nine o'clock – but who cared after the third martini?

Since Camp Pendleton was nearby, the marines became a major client base for Peto Motors. When the Third Marine Division moved to Okinawa, the bottom dropped out of the car market, and Uncle Fax struggled to make ends meet. He and Auntie Marge became Amway distributers in its first year. Again, Uncle Fax was a star salesman. He and Auntie Marge filled their garage to the brim with Amway products, worked the program, and became Diamond Direct leaders.

Marge Peto, 1974

Auntie Marge was a classy lady who was always dressed to the nines in her skirts and matching sweater sets. Her hair was done up and those *nails*, those bright red long shiny fingernails, were her trademark. She had a voice like music and a hug so warm and soft I could stay there all day.

Auntie Marge lived a long and rewarding life, and for that I am grateful. She was a warm and nurturing woman, and she gave me exactly what I missed at home. Even though she made her transition to the next world twenty five years ago, her bright and beautiful spirit shines on in her two wonderful daughters and especially in my heart. Her unconditional love sustained me and continues to nourish my soul.

Marjorie Elizabeth Jennings Peto
(1906 – 1976)

Addendum

Daughter Sandra Lee passed on Mother's Day 2013.

Sandra Lee Peto Schuster 1939 – 2013

Rest in peace my darlings.

7

Geraldine Ione Jennings Davis
(1908 – 1990)

Aunt Geri

Geraldine Ione Jennings, born 1908, was the middle child of five. She was a farm kid. Farming flows in the Jennings' veins.

Left to right: Thelma, Mother Lizzie, baby Byron Jr., Madge, Geraldine seated

Deep Creek School circa 1921 Geri: back row 3rd from left (in front of teacher), Madge: back row second in from right, Byron Jr: 2nd row, 6th from right

Geraldine went to Deep Creek School along with all the Jennings kids.

Geri 28, with brother Byron Jr. 26

Geraldine Jennings, age 25

Aunt Geri attended high school at Dominican in San Rafael with her sisters. She went to San Jose State, earning her degree and teaching credential about 1931. Three years later she married Eugene Pogue Davis in Fresno, California.

Remember Geraldine's mother, Lizzie Jennings, was also a Davis. That Davis line reaches all the way back to the Indian Creek Massacre in 1832. Furthermore Aunt Geri's grandmother, Sarah Ann Davis, was married to a Davis, Andrew Jackson Davis. On top of that Geri married Eugene Davis. All these Davises, yet none of the bloodlines cross. By some miracle no Davis in our family married a cousin.

My Dirty Dozen

Eugene Pogue Davis 1901 – 1990   *Uncle Gene Davis with his horse*

Uncle Gene was originally from Woodlake, California. After they were married in 1934, Gene and Geri lived in Visalia, where she taught fifth grade at Houston School. She also enjoyed gardening and sewing. Geraldine was one of the first to jump in and help when we had one of the famous reunions at Grandpa's ranch in the 1940's. Aunt Geri was good at everything she tried, and she was busy, busy, busy.

Uncle Gene owned and operated road-grading and surfacing equipment. He worked hard creating and repairing roads and highways. In 1940 their only child, Byron Jefferson Davis, came along. Everyone called him BJ as a child, but he insisted we call him Byron after he grew up. My cousin, BJ, was just about my age so I loved having the Davises around.

Aunt Geri

Byron Jefferson Davis, age 7

Jennings family reunion circa 1948

My Dirty Dozen

The Davis family decided to move to Canada in 1950. It must have taken months of planning, yet to me it seemed sudden. We went out to watch this amazing undertaking and to say goodbye. There was a seemingly endless parade of 'dozers, and scrapers, and graders, oh my! We said our goodbyes, and off they went like a herd of turtles, literally. Little by little they drove a long line of heavy equipment up Highway 198. This took hours. They travelled seventeen miles per hour, wide open. It took six weeks to make it to Beaverlodge, Alberta, Canada.

As a child I kept expecting the Davises to come back to California, but they never did. Because they were so far away, it wasn't possible to drop by for a spontaneous visit now and then. I wish I knew more to report about the Davis family. At least I will put down what I got from genealogy and my few faint memories.

After they got settled Aunt Geri set up shop in Beaverlodge, gardening during the two or three months when there was no snow. She eventually got a greenhouse and enjoyed her success with fruits and flowers in spite of the cold. Not unlike her father, Geraldine canned everything they didn't eat fresh. She was proud of her considerable accomplishments and talked about plants, sprouts, flowers and fruit all the time.

Aunt Geri

Aunt Geri in her garden in Beaverlodge, Alberta, Canada

Geri's son, Byron, married Gloria Jean Williams in 1964. They are still at the home place in Beaverlodge. Their three sons, Jeff, born in 1968, Tony in '71, and Barry in '74, have families of their own. Lane Thomas Davis is their one grandchild who was born in 1997. All three boys live at the ranch or in the vicinity.

Geraldine Davis in Beaverlodge, Alberta, with her brother, Byron Jennings Jr.

In 1983 my father, Byron, ventured up to Alberta to visit his sister one last time. They had been estranged since their father died in 1955. I have a feeling my father knew he should reach out to his sister to heal old wounds while there was time. His health was beginning to fail, and he passed away the next year.

Aunt Geri gave up the ghost in January of 1990. Her son, Byron, and wife, Gloria Jean, took care of Uncle Gene until he passed five months later. We just lost Gloria Jean this year, 2016. In any case the Davises were pioneers in their own right.

They are sorely missed.

Geraldine Ione Jennings Davis
(1908 – January 1990)

Eugene Pogue Davis
(1901 – May 1990)

Gloria Jean Williams Davis
(1941 – September 2016)

8

Thelma May Jennings Minnerly Farrar (1904 – 1999)

Aunt Thelma

Thelma May Jennings, age 8

Aunt Thelma was the eldest of the Jennings brood, having been born in 1904 to Byron Jennings Sr. and Elizabeth Davis Jennings.

Lizzie with her four oldest children: Thelma, standing to left, baby is Byron Jr.

Thelma attended Deep Creek School with her siblings. She must have graduated as she is not in the school photos in my collection. She was grown and gone before I came along. I wish I had more to report about Aunt Thelma. She deserves recognition for her accomplishments. As the eldest I bet she had many, but I simply don't know them.

Aunt Thelma was an energetic, adventurous sort. She attended Dominican High School and college in. Thelma was the only one in the family who stayed at Dominican for all of her secondary schooling. She was quite athletic and excelled in tennis.

Dominican High School, San Rafael, CA

My father told a story about a bank account the Jennings kids shared. I am not sure if they all contributed equally. I am guessing not as my father, Byron, was ten when Thelma was eighteen and away at school. The day came when Byron needed his share and went to the bank to draw it out. There was nothing in the account. He was furious and confronted his sister immediately. She refused to make it right. She had spent the money on new tennis togs, and had no intention of replacing it. This infuriated my father to such an extent that he hung on to his rage for decades. He called Thelma, "My lying sister." He was not kidding either.

The only time I saw Aunt Thelma was at family reunions at the ranch in the 1940's.

Family reunion at Jennings' ranch circa 1948, Thelma back row 2nd from left

At age 22 Thelma married Clarence Minnerly in Salt Lake City. Four years later they moved to Twin Falls, Idaho, where their two sons, Clarence Minnerly Jr. (1928) and James William Minnerly (1930) were born.

Clarence Minnerly Jr., paratrooper   *James William Minnerly (Corky) age 3*

Thelma divorced Clarence after six years of marriage. Not long after, she sailed to Hawaii. Thelma had been single for nine years when she met and married Raleigh Farrar. For some reason they tied the knot in Oregon. After seven years she headed back to Hawaii. Aunt Thelma and Uncle Raleigh returned to Visalia for family reunions in the late 1940's.

Thelma kept the ship lines busy making trips back and forth between Hawaii and California in 1949 and 1950. She managed to squeeze in time to live in Ketchikan, Alaska, as well as Subic Bay, Philippines. She settled down in Honolulu, Hawaii, around 1980.

Aunt Thelma

Thelma Jennings Minnerly Farrar, about age 40

While Thelma travelled she asked her youngest sister, Elizabeth, who lived in Visalia, to take care of her sons, Clarence and Corky, who were toddlers. Since Elizabeth had no children of her own, she was glad to take part in raising her nephews. She was a second mother to those boys. She kept them up to speed on the social graces. They also learned the value of hard work and industriousness. Attentive parenting by Elizabeth paid off as Clarence grew up to be the most financially successful member of the entire Jennings clan. He was a major real estate developer in exclusive Los Gatos of the 1960s. Clarence later owned and operated a 1,000 acre almond orchard in Delano along with a large packinghouse. He and his wife, Ann, settled in an exclusive estate in Montecito, outside of Santa Barbara.

Clarence's brother, Corky? I have no clue. I have not seen him since we were kids. I don't even know the story behind that nick-name. I have made several attempts to contact him to no avail, even though he lives in San Francisco.

In her later years Aunt Thelma moved to Montecito and was cared for by her son, Clarence, and his family. She passed away in 1999 at the age of 94.

Thelma May Jennings Minnerly
(1904 – 1999)

9
Benjamin Bartlett Fisher
(1882 – 1960)
Grandpa Fisher

Benjamin Bartlett Fisher

My mother's father, Benjamin Fisher, was a dour sort of man, introverted, quiet, with anger bubbling just under the surface. Even so, he held me in highest esteem as the oldest of his five grandchildren. He always had a roll of Five Flavor Lifesavers in his right pants pocket, He gently peeled back the paper for me to pick one. I was happy with just one candy with no thought of asking for more.

Benjamin Bartlett Fisher was born in southern Kentucky near the Tennessee border in 1882 to James Harrison Fisher and Martha Savilla Jo Peden. They called her Mattie Fisher. Ben was the sixth of eight brothers and sisters. Remember this – Benjamin's next older sister was Martha but they called her Mattie.

Glasgow, Kentucky, was a small village of fewer than 200 residents at the time. There were not many potential mates to choose from. It was not as if they could jump in the car and visit friends 50 miles away, or even 20 miles. They had no car. Automobiles had yet to be manufactured for the common man. Such a visit via horse-drawn carriage was a major undertaking and rarely happened. A mile or so across town, however, lived the Eaton family consisting of Harrison Riley Eaton and his wife Martha Hunt, another Mattie, and four kids. The oldest was Gertrude. Sadly Harrison's wife, Martha Hunt Eaton, died at age 30 leaving him with a house full of kids. He wasted no time finding a mother for those kids when he married Martha Fisher from the Fisher family across town. Clever move, Harrison. Your second wife had the same name as your first – Mattie Eaton.

Grandpa Fisher

Benjamin Fisher was only 17 when his sister Martha married into the Eaton family. She became the second wife of Harrison, the father, Gertrude Eaton, my grandma. She was only ten, but Ben had his eye on this eldest Eaton girl. When Gertrude turned 16 he married her. He married his sister's step-daughter in 1905. He was 23, and she only 16. They moved to California in 1908. I wonder what possessed them to make such a drastic move. I can only guess that they decided to escape the shenanigans of Kentucky and make a fresh start.

Ben and Gertrude Fisher wedding

To further complicate matters a common nick-name for Martha was Mattie. There are so many Marthas, and Matties, and Harrisons it's giving me a headache. Harrison and the second Mattie Eaton proceeded to have seven more children. Wisely there is not a Martha or a Harrison in the bunch.

My Dirty Dozen

*Mammoth Cave, Kentucky, BB Fisher 3rd row right in suspenders.
Gertie, top row right.
The short lady back row right could be Mattie Fisher, Ben's sister.*

When Harrison died in 1926, Mattie became a widow when she was only 47. I assume she had no means of support and was dependent on the family for the rest of her life. The US census shows her living in Lindsay, CA, with my grandparents Ben and Gertie (sister/step-mother). And then at age 80 records show Mattie living the remainder of her life in Taylorville, IL, with daughter, Mary Nutt. She passed away at age 86 in Taylorville, surrounded by family.

I discovered the picture of Mammoth Cave in my huge cache of family photos and realized my grandparents are in it. There is no caption or inscription. I bet they took in this attraction when they were picking up Mattie to bring her to California, or maybe it was when they delivered her to Illinois later in life.

The family took care of its own. Within a couple of years of coming to California, Grandpa and Grandma took in Ben's younger brother, George Washington Fisher, who worked in a packing house and later trimming and budding trees. George was drafted into the army during WW I. He never married and lived out his days alone in Dinuba, California.

Ben's eldest brother, John Logan Fisher, established his home in Taylorville, Illinois, near his sister, Mary, and the state capital, Springfield. With only a fourth grade education John managed to own and operate a substantial farm. He also took in his 25 year old sister, Mary, and later his 55 year old brother, Sina Radford Fisher.

This photo with the faint inscription "El Festino" is of Ben and Gertie in front of their rented farm house in Lindsay, California.

While the census lists El Festino as rented, I assume Benjamin, as the superintendent of a large fruit farm, was provided housing as a benefit of employment. The 1920 census lists nine Japanese and Italian farm workers at the same residence in Lindsay. I wonder if Grandma was in charge of feeding those workers along with her own two children and her step-mother.

Farmer, Ben, in California

Fisher home place in Exeter

Ben successfully managed vineyards and orchards for Pinkham Properties for many years. He saved enough to purchase a small twenty acre vineyard on the Exeter/Farmersville road. For the rest of his life he tended that vineyard. He and Grandma had chickens, blackberry bushes, and sweet peas.

My clearest memory of Grandpa Fisher was sitting in his upright chair in the living room holding in his lap the biggest book I had ever seen. It was the Bible, and he read silently from the Old Testament as the family milled around him. I wonder if his very strong sense of judgment and criticism might have come from the Good Book. He rarely uttered an opinion out loud. Sometimes there was a grunt or hum – "hm-hmmm." Nobody knew what it meant, except Grandma. She came in from the kitchen and explained.

"He said, Joe is a liar!" or

"Doris is a busy body!"

It was always some judgment. You could never get him to elaborate. He just made his sounds, and then withdrew.

The warmest times in that house were the Thanksgiving and Christmas gatherings with aunts, uncles and cousins running around. Amidst the hubbub Grandpa sat silently in his upright chair holding his Bible.

My mother, Mary, remembers watching her father, explode many a time when she was little. Once he slammed the back screen door so hard, it fell off the hinges. I never saw that side of him, but on some level I was aware of it, as I never talked back to Grandpa Fisher.

I remember his green DeSoto. He kept that car spotless. It had one of the first automatic transmissions, called a *fluid drive*. He had to accelerate and then back off the gas to get it to shift. That was quite the challenge. Whenever we were in the car, we all held our breaths and hoped it would actually move to the next gear by this strange method.

1950 De Soto with Fluid Drive

One of the first cloverleaf interchanges to a highway was constructed near our house on Highway 198 and the Farmersville Boulevard. Every time we came to that circular entrance Grandpa got mad. "Why do I have to turn north, when I want to go south?" he complained loudly. He had a hard time adjusting to anything new. "Why do I have to turn north, when I want to go south?" he complained loudly. He had a hard time adjusting to anything new.

Full cloverleaf exchange - The cloverleaf in question only has two leaves (partial)

I was a kid who took a nap every afternoon until I started school. One summer I went down for my nap, and when I awoke, there was a brand new swing. To this day I don't know how Grandpa made that swing for me in only an hour while I slept. It was not just two ropes on a tree either. He built a big sturdy wood frame, whitewashed it, and attached two strong chains, and a metal tractor seat.

Showing my new swing to neighbor

Happy Anne in her swing

I was surprised and delighted. My Grandpa must have loved me a lot to have made me such a wonderful gift. I spent hours and hours on that swing. My friends and my brother made up games to play on it. One person took a turn swinging, while the other ran across in front to see how close he could come without getting hit. Well, the inevitable happened. That iron tractor seat clipped me in the chin, and it bled like crazy. I still have that scar.

My Dirty Dozen

We enjoyed many events together as a family: rodeos, horse shows, games, concerts and more. One of our favorites was baseball. Mother, Daddy, Brother Bill, and I were avid baseball fans. We attended every home game of the Visalia Cubs, a C-class farm team, for the Chicago Cubs organization. We usually had dinner before the game at our favorite Mexican restaurant, Las Palmas. Rooting for our favorite team in the cool evening air was one of those sweet family pleasures after a hot valley day.

We were always trying to persuade Grandma and Grandpa Fisher to go with us. Grandpa was resistant to the idea. When pressed as to why, he told us he was afraid a ball might hit him. Nobody really took that seriously. We begged and pleaded with Grandpa and eventually he agreed to go with us, but he was not happy. By then we were able to afford box seats, so the 50-foot high wire screen was right in front of our faces. Everybody was having a grand ol' time except for Grandpa, who was shaking with fear. It was the fourth inning, and the batter hit a foul ball down the third base line. The ball soared high, high in the air and looped right over the top of that tall screen and came down squarely on Grandpa's shoulder. I mean what are the odds? Grandpa was badly hurt, and we had to take him home. This ended his bout with baseball. It makes me wonder if Grandpa foresaw this fluke of fate.

Grandpa Fisher

My father managed to score a couple of tickets to the World Series in Cleveland in 1954. The Indians lost in four games to the NY Giants, but that's not my point. Mother and Daddy flew back to Cleveland. Grandma and Grandpa stayed with Bill and me while they were gone.

I will never forget this. The four of us were at the dinner table. I said, "I wonder how Mother and Daddy are doing." Grandpa's face turned bright red, scrunched up, and he burst out crying. I had never seen this before. Of course Grandpa didn't explain, but Grandma came to the rescue. She said,
"He knows that it is impossible for that much metal to fly in the air, and they are going to crash. He figured they were already dead." He did not believe airplanes or trust doctors either.

He had a hernia for as long as I can remember. He refused to let a doctor touch him, so he wore a truss most of his life instead. I didn't understand the mechanics of the device at the time. I figured it was some kind of uncomfortable belt he wore under his clothing. It was one of those embarrassing subjects that one avoided. Even without medical care Grandpa lasted 78 years. He and Grandma celebrated their Golden Wedding anniversary in 1957 three years before he passed.

My Dirty Dozen

Ben and Gertie's Golden Wedding Anniversary 1957
Note his adoring look at her

Ben was a fiercely independent man. He had a laser-like focus and refused to stop until the job was complete. These qualities held him in good stead as a breadwinner. He may have been fighting internal demons most his life, but for the most part, he was able to keep them in check. He trusted only his tight inner circle and was suspicious of everyone else. In spite of these considerable obstacles, he worked hard, he played fair, and he provided for his family to the best of his ability. He loved and was loved in return. Two children and five grandchildren are a fitting legacy for a job well done. We all turned out, Grandpa. Thanks for all you did and all you were.

Benjamin Fisher Taken By Death

Benjamin B. Fisher, 78, resident of Tulare Count for more than 50 years, die this morning in an Exete hospital after a lengthy il ness.

Mr. Fisher, a retired ranch er, was born in Glasgow, Ky. where he attended school He was married to the for mer Gertrude Eaton in 1907 The following year the) moved to California, settlin; first in Lindsay.

Four years later, the) moved to the Exeter area.

Mr. Fisher had been re tired for the last 20 years. He had been in ill health for about five years.

In addition to his widow, he is survived by a son, Ed ward Stephen Fisher of Exe er; a daughter, Mrs. Mary Jennings of Visalia; a broth r, Rad Fisher of Taylorville, Ill.; a sister, Mrs. J. H. Nutt, also of Taylorville; and five grandchildren.

Funeral services will be Friday at 2 p.m. in the Had ey Funeral Chapel in Exe er with the Rev. Cecil W. Johnson officiating. Burial vill be in the Exeter Ceme ery.

Benjamin Bartlett Fisher
(1882 – 1960)

My Dirty Dozen

The Trailblazers
Grandma Fisher's People

Before I talk about Grandma Fisher I want to share some interesting tidbits about her ancestors that I stumbled upon while researching. Naysa Simmons and his wife Sally Stephens were buried in a family plot located in Fountain Run, Kentucky, in 1859. The plot was in disrepair, and all the stones were down except two, Naysa's and Sally's. In 1939 a distant relative, Clyde Clayton Simmons, discovered the Kentucky family burial site of my great-great-great-great-grandparents.

Simmons private graveyard, 1859

Clyde did what he could to clean it up. He figured if nothing more was done, the family graveyard would be lost forever. At that time what was left of the house was occupied by Naysa's great-grandson, Will Russell. That was 75 years ago.

Naysa Simmons, originally from North Carolina, moved to Kentucky in 1805 where he married a local girl, Sarah Stephens (Sally). They settled in a small town now known as Fountain Run. It is in the southern part of the state, near Nashville, Tennessee.

Naysa acquired a lot of land and a number of slaves. Records show that he purchased two tracts of land from Samuel Parker in 1817. He traded a horse for another tract of land. In those days horses were of great value. The previous owner of the land had struggled to survive in the Kentucky wilderness, so he took the horse and returned home to the East.

The Simmons family built a two-story log house on their property. Fountain Run Baptist Church was organized in their home. Services were held there until a proper church could be erected. Remnants of a still were found behind the Simmons' house. Gentlemen of a better class frequently made their own whisky in those days. Naysa, like many other Kentucky gentlemen, kept wines and liquors in his cellar. Occasions were often celebrated with great hilarity in the Simmons house. Naysa had taken to "imbibing of the flowing bowl" to the extent that he was constantly being brought before the church for his transgressions; however the elders decided to keep Naysa in good standing because he was a gentleman and because of his generous tithing.

Naysa and Sally's daughter, Martha (Patsy) Simmons, married John Hunt. Like his father-in-law, John hailed from North Carolina where he received his early education. He moved to Barren County, Kentucky, as a young man. John purchased some wild land and cleared and cultivated it. Hunt and his wife, Patsy, were also devoted church members. They attended the Missionary Baptist Church.

John's father, Jonathan Hunt, also from North Carolina, soon followed his son to Kentucky. The Hunt family engaged in agriculture until John's death in 1855. Jonathan Hunt was a Revolutionary War veteran, having served under General Morgan in the Carolinas. He was taken prisoner several times, according to official records.

In those days families did not venture far from home. In five generations the Simmons/Hunt clan managed to migrate five miles north to Tracy, Kentucky. Tracy was an unincorporated village in the days of my ancestors. Today, it so small that the census does not measure it separately. Population is estimated at 200. Fountain Run population is at 213. Eventually my family ended up in Glasgow, sixteen miles north, where my grandmother, Gertie, was born. Five generations later, Grandma broke with tradition and came out to California with her husband, Ben Fisher.

My Dirty Dozen

10

Gertrude Ethyl Eaton Fisher
(1889 – 1995)

Grandma Fisher

She drew her first breath in 1889 in Glasgow, Kentucky. Her parents named Gertrude Ethyl Eaton, but they called her Gertie. I called her Grandma.

Tintype of Gertrude Eaton 1889

Gertrude, Mamie, Levie, and Ida were the children of Harrison and Mattie Eaton. Unfortunately Mattie Eaton died when Gertrude, the eldest, was 10. Harrison, my great grandfather, must have been overwhelmed with a litter of kids and no wife. He wasted no time finding a second wife and married her in less than a year. Her name was Martha Fisher, nicknamed Mattie! Wait, his first wife was Mattie. At least he didn't have to worry about calling her by the wrong name. That was the easy part.

Stranger than fiction:

Gertrude's father's given name was Harrison. My Grandpa Benjamin's father was James Harrison. Gertrude had a brother named Levie. Benjamin had a brother named Levy. Gertrude had a sister named Mamie. Benjamin had a sister named Mary but they called her Mamie. Harrison Eaton, married Mattie Eaton (Gertrude's parents). After Mattie died he married Martha Fisher but they called her Mattie. I don't expect you to follow all of that or even some of it. It is still amazing and part of my story.

On with Gertrude...

Benjamin and Gertrude back in Kentucky

Grandma Fisher

Grandma was a tiny woman of five feet, and wore a size five shoe. She always wore one of those torturous lace-up corsets. We called her bust-line her cookie-shelf. She thought that was funny. Her hugs were warm and pillow-like. Grandma was a wonderful cook, making everything from scratch. She healed every boo-boo with a hug and a cookie.

Gertie, my Grandma, married Ben, my Grandpa, when she was 16. Ben and Gertie set up housekeeping in Glasgow, Kentucky. Both the Fishers and the Eatons lived in Glasgow. There is even an Eaton cemetery there. I was never privy to the reason they came out to California. They were not the adventurous type. Maybe it was for health reasons or weather, or maybe it was for a job. Ben landed a good position as the superintendent of Pinkham Properties, the largest ranch in Lindsay, California.

It was five years after they married before Mary, my mother, was born and two more years until Steven Fisher, my uncle, came along. Unlike the rest of the Fishers and Eatons, they stopped after two children. They saved for years in order to purchase their own small vineyard and home in Exeter, California around 1920. This is the house I remember when I think of Grandma.

Grandma and Grandpa's house in Exeter, CA

Gertrude and Benjamin Fisher wed 1906

Gertie with her first-born, Mary, my mother

Ben, Gertie, Mary, Steve

Grandma's cranberry relish was always a hit. We loved it when she prepared the entire Christmas dinner, of course. But when my mother and I took the reins, we begged for Grandma to bring her cranberry relish. Using only fresh ingredients, she ground the cranberries in an old cast-iron meat grinder. It was secured to the counter with a thumb screw and had a large crank.

Grandma's grinder

Round and round she worked, grinding those berries and always added her secret ingredient, an orange. She didn't skimp on the sugar, either. Eventually my mother learned the recipe and passed it on to me. I have made Grandma's cranberry relish for years. Even as a guest, I offer to bring cranberry relish as my contribution, so I can tell Grandma's story.

One year I was at Albertsons gathering ingredients for Thanksgiving. I grabbed the bag of fresh cranberries. I don't know what possessed me to look on the bag, but I did. Right there on the Ocean Spray bag was my grandmother's recipe. First I was deflated, then I was mad, and then I realized, it's the story. The story is the best part, and it was ruined. That

My Dirty Dozen

night I told the story for the last time. You know what my dear friends concluded? Ocean Spray must have snapped up that recipe from your Grandmother. We all agreed, so now I tell the story every year remembering Grandma fondly.

Both Grandma and Grandpa looked forward to the Kentucky Picnic held at Mooney Grove in Visalia every year. It was the one chance to connect with people from back home.

Kentucky Picnic, Gertie and Ben 2nd row

Gertie was active about town. In 1949 she became a charter member of the Exeter Woman's Club. It continues to provide for the civic and social interests of its members. The Club still meets on the second Wednesday of the month at the Exeter Library, 65 years later.

She belonged to Neighbors of Woodcraft, which was the ladies' auxiliary to the Woodmen of the World. These were fraternal orders complete with secret rituals and passwords.

More importantly, for a small premium the Neighbors of Woodcraft provided life insurance for its members. This was designed to prevent widows from becoming destitute if the breadwinner died. The death benefit was somewhere between $500 and $2000. This would have been enough to pay off the farm with some left over for living expenses. We think that the saying, "He bought the farm," (meaning "he died") originated with these insurance policies.

I'm sure Gertie contributed her share to the Exeter Garden club. She was a natural when it came to plants. I remember a ten-foot-tall row of blackberries full of sharp thorns and sweet berries. My taste buds were spoiled for rasberries or olallieberries. They are just not as good as my Grandma's. Her sweetpeas were heavenly. She planted on Christmas Day. I received a drop of sweetpea in my DNA. You will find the granddaughter version in front of my house every spring.

Anne's sweetpeas

My Dirty Dozen

Fisher Golden Wedding anniversary

Grandma and Grandpa celebrated their Golden Wedding anniversary in 1957. My mother and Aunt Mil put on a nice party for them at our house in Farmersville. Dear friends and relatives attended. They had food and gifts, and my clarinet quartet from school provided the entertainment.

After Grandpa died in 1960, Grandma carried on for another 25 years until she succumbed at age 96. The doctors said she had a strong heart and lungs which kept her going. I think her diet of fresh foods from the garden with nothing artificial helped too. Also Grandma was a simple woman, who looked on the bright side. She was way ahead of the happiness movement and Oprah's gratitude journal.

When she was nearing the end, she lived in a facility near my house in Visalia. Once a week I gathered my son from school, swung by Baskin Robbins and picked up three milkshakes, one for Grandma, of course, one for me, and one for Robert. We sat on the side of the bed and visited while we slurped.

Grandma liked music. She loved the times I brought my guitar and sang a few old folk songs for her. Often times she chimed in with her high, thin voice, right on pitch. She remembered all the words, to "Old Joe Clark" or "You Get a Line and I'll Get a Pole, Honey."

There were so many simple yet meaningful moments with Grandma. She was soft and warm and I always felt safe when I was with her. She was my only Grandma, and I was her special girl. I knew she was proud of me and that meant a lot.

She was my Grandma.

We were connected and

we still are.

My Dirty Dozen

In Memory of:	Gertrude Ethel Fisher
Born:	October 14, 1889 Glasgow, Kentucky
Died:	September 25, 1986 Visalia, California
Survived by:	Her Son Steve Fisher Five Grandchildren Five Great Grandchildren
Preceded in Death by:	Her Son, Benjamin Fisher Her Daughter, Mary Fisher Jennings
Graveside Services at:	10:00 O'Clock in the Morning Tuesday, September 30, 1986 Exeter Cemetery, Exeter, Cal.
Officiating:	Pastor John Epp, Retired First Baptist Church Visalia, California
Member of:	Exeter Womens Club Exeter Garden Club Neighbors of the Woodcraft
Interment:	Next to her Husband Benjamin Fisher Who Passed away November 16, 1960 Exeter Cemetery, Exeter, Calif.

Gertrude Ethyl Eaton Fisher
(1889 – 1985)

11

Edward Stephen Fisher
(1913 – 1991)

Mildred Virginia Brown Fisher
(1923 – 1992)

Uncle Steve and Aunt Mil

Uncle Steve was just two years younger than my mother. She was born on the 12th and he was born on the 10th of October. Both kids were birthday gifts for their mother whose birthday was October 14th.

Mary, 29 and Steve, 27 – San Francisco

Uncle Steve didn't talk much. I got the feeling there was something simmering just beneath the surface. His daughters told me one time he got so mad he shattered a plate against the wall. This is reminiscent of his father, Benjamin, slamming the screen door off the hinges. The fruit didn't fall far from the tree.

Edward Stephen Fisher as a young man

Steve graduated from Exeter High School in 1930 and went to Visalia Junior College for a couple years. He played football in college in spite of his small stature. Once a ball hit him square in the eye and severely damaged his sight. I know he suffered with back pain most of his life, which was probably the result of a gridiron accident, too.

Steve had just one job his entire life, field manager for Nash de Camp, a large packing house in the Valley. Changing jobs was not an option in Steve's mind. He was out and about visiting one ranch or another for forty years. One of the large ranches he serviced was Pinkham Properties in Exeter, CA. Remember his father, Ben Fisher, was a superintendent for Pinkham Properties when Steve was growing up. One time when Steve moseyed into the Pinkham office, a new secretary caught his eye. He found out her name was Mildred Brown, and he hung around hoping to get to know this new girl.

Pinkham Farms Office

Mildred Brown in Coast Guard

Mildred always wanted to be a hair dresser, but her mother would not allow her to pursue such a low-class trade. Her mother was pleased after Pearl Buck, a close family friend, secured for Mildred a secretarial position with Pinkham Properties. Mildred was not happy there and quit that job to join the Coast Guard in defiance of her mother. Uncle Steve was not thrilled about this development but did not let this complication deter him. The Coast Guard sent Mil to Florida. Steve followed her there. Then she was transferred to Washington state. The family always claimed Steve chased Mil until she let him catch her. They were married on Halloween, 1944, in Seattle, Washington.

Before long James Michael Fisher was born in 1946. Cousins, Jimmy and my brother Bill were born only weeks apart. This made for a slew of comparisons both good and not so good, such as

"Jimmy is the smart one" and

"Bill is the athletic one."

Such so-called compliments cut both ways. It was praise with a hook.

Steve, Mil, and baby Jimmy

Steve and Jimmy playing horsey, ranch north of Exeter

After Jim, Steve and Mil were blessed with twin girls, Caroline and Catherine, making their family complete. They cleverly named them Caroline Thomasina, and Catherine Stephanie. We called them Tommy and Stevie until they were old enough to put a stop to that.

Caroline, Jimmy and Catherine

Aunt Mil was one of those women who managed to keep lots of plates in the air all the time. She was a good cook, a great seamstress, fabulous at needlework, and she raised three kids. Once the twins were in the eighth grade, Mildred went to work as a bookkeeper.

Uncle Steve

When we dropped by, Aunt Mil was always busy. Even when she relaxed she was knitting or crocheting some project. I was fascinated by this and sat by her to watch. Before long she had me set up with a skein of yarn and some needles. She demonstrated how to cast on, and knit and purl. She went back to her knitting, and I struggled along at about one row to her four, but I was hooked. Next time I saw her, I proudly displayed my progress, and then she taught me something new. This was our special relationship.

Mildred was not admired by her in-laws. Grandpa Fisher ridiculed her behind her back. He claimed she was bossy and didn't know her place as a woman. Uncle Steve visited his parents every Wednesday, but Aunt Mil was not welcome. Steve could bring Jimmy however, who was Grandpa's favorite. He called Jimmy, "My Little Man." When the twin girls came to visit, Grandma pulled out pictures of Steve's early girlfriend, saying, "Isn't she a lot prettier than Mildred?" I never understood that kind of treatment. Aunt Mil was not terribly warm but to me she was so capable and generous. I looked up to her.

My Dirty Dozen

Steve Fisher in his mother's yard

Steve and Mil were two peas in a pod. They both worked hard and saved. They upgraded from the modest ranch house in the country to a nice place in Exeter.

136 N. Crespi, Exeter, CA

In a few more years they moved to a lovely home in Visalia with a pool.

3323 W. Howard, Visalia, CA

When Grandma Fisher was declining, Aunt Mil cared for her. Eventually they moved Grandma into their spare bedroom in Visalia. Mildred fed Grandma, cleaned up after her, and cared for her for years. At one point they hired a nurse to help with Grandma. Nevertheless it was a difficult, thankless job. Sometimes Aunt Mil complained, but she took care of her mother-in-law anyway. I imagine she did it as a labor of love for her husband.

In retirement Steve and Mil golfed, and travelled in their RV with a group called the Senior Gadabouts. They drove as far as New England to see the fall leaves. They got a kick out of taking cruises, such as the one through the Panama Canal. They decided to live it up, and live it up they did. They earned it.

Uncle Steve logged hundreds of thousands of miles driving for work, not to mention all that travelling in retirement. His eyesight was not good, and he had a bad back, but he never complained. One day Steve dropped by his daughter, Caroline's house, to mow her lawn. On his way home the unthinkable happened. Either he blacked out, was distracted, or blinded briefly, and he plowed into a car at an intersection. Everyone was all right except Uncle Steve who suffered a head injury.

Like his father, Steve didn't trust doctors. He said he felt fine and went home after the accident. We don't know what happened medically. He seemed to be on the mend. A few months later he mysteriously got dizzy and fell into a coma. This time they took him to Kaweah Delta Hospital in Visalia. In a few days he woke up and asked for ice cream. It was a miracle! On July 1, 1991, the family congregated only to find he lapsed back into a coma. This time he failed to wake up.

Some described Steve as bull-headed and stubborn like his father. Once offended, he never forgave the person. I remember Uncle Steve as a good man who worked hard and did the right thing. His life was cut short at age seventy-eight.

After Steve was gone, life was not the same for Aunt Mil. She had lost her kindred spirit of forty-six years. She carried on as long as she could, but she succumbed on December, 28, the following year, 1992. Both Uncle Steve and Aunt Mil were an integral part of our family and are sorely missed.

Edward Stephen Fisher
(1913 – 1991)

Mildred Virginia Brown Fisher
(1923 – 1992)

My Dirty Dozen

12

Byron William Jennings III
(1946 – 1997)

Brother Bill

His name was Byron William Jennings III, but let's face it there were simply too many Byrons, so they settled on Bill. Setting the stage for what was to come, take a look at this precious boy. He was one unhappy cowboy.

Bill, age 4 – He loved that cowboy suit, boots and hat.

Bill, Grades 1-6

My Dirty Dozen

Bill was a darling blond with a quick wit. He was a clever kid, excelling in academics and sports. The deportment (behavior) grade was another story. In spite of his shenanigans he was popular with kids and grownups alike.

He was born in Kaweah Delta Hospital in Visalia, where I was born and where Byron Jr, our father, was born. Since children were not allowed in the hospital, my father needed to stay with me, so there we were outside the hospital on our horses. Judging by the time of year, October 3, it must have been the Tulare County Fair parade. Daddy and I always rode in parades and horse shows. My father was on his beautiful bay, and I was on that rascal, Corny, my Shetland pony. Mother was inside in labor, and we were outside in a parade. Does that seem right? At the time I was perfectly happy to ride in a parade with my Daddy.

October 3, 1946, Kaweah Delta Hospital – Byron and Anne in foreground

What a gift for Mother, to have a son born nine days before her birthday in 1946. They finally got their boy. My parents announced the arrival by flying a flag in the front yard. But this was no ordinary flag. It was a diaper that had been dyed blue. The pole was originally a walnut shaking pole, a long wooden pole with a hook on the end used to shake walnuts off the tree.

Bill Jennings, III, Birth Announced

The blue flag flying from a pole in the yard of Mr. and Mrs. B. W. Jennings, Jr., of East Sierra boulevard, is one of Bill the third's three cornered pants borrowed from his layette to celebrate his arrival on Oct. 3 at the Visalia hospital.

The young man, who carries on the name for a third generation of a pioneer family of this community, weighed 8 pounds, 2 ounces at birth. He has a big sister, Anne, aged 5½ years.

Mrs. Jennings is the former Mary Fisher, daughter of Mr. and Mrs. B. B. Fisher, of a long-time Exeter family. Mr. B. W. Jennings, Sr., is paternal grandfather.

Bill's birth announcement

Walnut pole flying blue diaper in front yard

Father and son

My Dirty Dozen

Bill under Mother's arm

Bill was a prized package. He was never out of Mother's sight. She just threw him under her arm and went about her business. Bill was a product of the highly popular *Dr. Spock's Baby and Child Care* book which came out in 1946, the year he was born. Spock encouraged parents to see their children as individuals and not to apply a one-size-fits all philosophy to them.

During my childhood experts advised parents that babies needed to sleep on a regular schedule. They should not pick them up and hold them whenever they cried. That taught them to cry more and not sleep through the night. Further they were told to feed their children on a regular schedule and not coddle them.

The contrast in child-rearing methods in five years was dramatic. I was raised the old way, which contributed to my independence and strong work ethic. Bill was quite the opposite. He prided himself in achieving maximum reward for minimum work. In five short years a new generation was born. Hard work was no longer in vogue, giving rise to the free-spirit-generation. I wonder if we should blame Dr. Spock.

Anne and Bill on Corny – Daddy standing

Our father did everything to make Bill into a cowboy like the rest of the family. He parked him on Corny with me. Mother dressed him like a cowboy, and they bought him his own horse. He called his horse the first name that came to mind, Trigger, but he didn't want to ride. He didn't want to feed the horses. He simply was not interested in this family tradition.

The only photo in existence of Bill on Trigger

Prior to my brother's birth my parents did a great job preparing me for the new arrival. I was excited and ready for him. Naturally, I wanted to hold my new brother, but it was over a year before they allowed this cherished child in my arms. I wasn't jealous at first, but if our folks wanted to ease the sibling rivalry, this was not the way to do it. My feelings were hurt. I felt they loved him more.

Brother Bill

Anne holding Bill after a year

They finally let me hold my brother, but by then, the groundwork for battle had been laid. In a few years I was expected to watch Bill – without pay of course. This put a damper on my social life, not to mention the fact that I was always running the risk of his tattling. That added another layer of resentment. We competed for everything, but since I was bigger, I usually won. By then his anger was brewing too. Quite frequently we erupted into physical battles. Typically I grabbed him behind the neck with thumb and forefinger and pinched hard with my nails. He kicked me in the shins with his hard-soled boots. I always had silver dollar-sized bruises on my shins. I imagine he had red marks on his neck. If our parents got involved, we both got spanked, no questions asked. Needless to say we learned to keep a lid on our conflicts and inflict injury on the QT.

My Dirty Dozen

Can that opened with a key

Once we fought over a can of shoestring potatoes. This type of can, when open, had a razor-sharp rim. We chased around the table and wrestled trying to get the can from each other. The sharp can sliced Bill's upper arm and it bled all over the place. When I realized he was seriously hurt, I was genuinely worried and remorseful. I didn't want to hurt my brother, I just wanted to win. It was a relief that he was all right.

His perspective was quite different. He believed I was always against him. He harbored that grudge into adulthood. Once I found out how he felt, I tried to explain and smooth it over, but it was too late. He didn't believe me. Sibling rivalry is normal, but this was too much. Our parents, had they been more tuned in, might have eased the growing tension between Bill and me.

Our relationship improved once Bill became a teenager and we had a few interests in common. I taught him to jitterbug. Once we even took a road trip together. My friends liked Bill, which made the babysitting chore easier and more agreeable.

Bill was athletic, excelling at baseball, football and golf.

Little League minors Byron Jr., top left, Bill 2nd from right

Little League Majors – Bill, 2nd row, 2nd from left

Our father was so proud, he was at every game. He was even on the Little League Board of Directors.

My Dirty Dozen

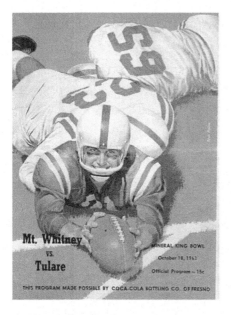

Oct.18, 1963 official program

Bill Jennings

Bill, 11th grade – inside program

JAYCEE CHAMPIONS — Santa Ana College won the team title and Terry McCabe of Fresno City College, kneeling, middle, the individual title in the third annual Far Western Junior College Golf Championships. Top row, from left, Santa Ana Coach Arlin Pirtle, Ken Sutherland, Norbert Loehnig, Tom Killeen, Ray Carrasco, Rick Divel and Jerry Sheffield. Kneeling, Dave Sabo of Fresno CC, first handicap flight winner; McCabe, and Byron Jennings of College of the Sequoias, second handicap flight winner.

COS Golf Team April 1965, Byron Jennings III, kneeling on right

Brother Bill

When my brother entered college, he had made up his mind that the name "Bill" wouldn't work any longer. He refused to be called something that comes in the mail and you have to pay every month. He insisted everyone call him "Byron." Look, I was his big sister and used the name "Bill" for 18 years. I was not about to change. Eventually he refused to respond. I guess that's one I didn't win.

A lot of changes occurred in 1960 while I was away at San Jose State. Our mother was shuffled off to Kings View mental hospital. Our parents launched into a vicious divorce, their assets were divided, and Dad moved out. My brother was stuck at home, while I came home for summers and holidays. When we spent time with Mother, we were betraying our father. When we were with Dad, Mother was hurt. There was no way for us kids to win. It was not a happy time.

My Dad was never able to manage without a woman. Remember when Mother did all the shopping for him? After the separation he wasted no time finding someone else. It was not long until our father met Pamela Hessler in a bar in Fresno. In 1965 I landed a job teaching in the Far East. While I was in Okinawa I got a telegram from my father, **"CONGRATULATIONS IN ORDER [STOP] MARRIED MAY 31 VENTURA [STOP] ALL IS WELL [STOP] LOVE DAD AND PAMELA"**. Nobody let me know they were planning to marry. Nobody sent me an invitation. Nobody called me with the good news. I did not receive a letter. I was sent an impersonal telegram to notify me that they were already married. To add insult to injury my brother stood up as the best man. I felt kicked out of my own family. It was horrible.

I stayed overseas, and my brother went to UCLA. We both needed to get away.

During this period young men were being drafted left and right. Byron wisely postponed his academic goals and avoided the draft. He headed to Europe for an extended back-packing trip. By then I had been transferred to Wiesbaden, Germany, with the Department of Defense Overseas Dependent Schools (DODODS). Housing was provided as part of the benefit package. We teachers were given a single room in a WWII hotel with a shared bathroom. This was my only home for the two years I was in Germany. My brother came to visit me while I was there. He slept on the floor with his head in the closet. That was all the room I had. We had a lot of good times during his stay. The military did not share our sense of fun. I kept getting notice after notice to contact the company commander in my mail box. I knew I was getting reprimanded for something, so I cavalierly tossed those edicts. Finally an M.P. (Military Police) knocked on my door late one night, asking for my brother's passport. They did not know my male friend was my brother. They assumed I was co-habitating, which was against their many rules. We had no intention of clarifying the situation either. Why on earth would they be suspicious of a long haired male with a beard spending the night in my room? He stuck out like a sore thumb in that clean-cut military community. I suppose it did look bad. Finally Byron left, and at the end of the school year I left. Neither of us were cut out for the restrictive military life. We were too much *Jennings*.

Byron and Mike Wells

When Byron got back from Europe, he hightailed it to Mexico with his best friend Mike Wells. (Mike's father, Scotty, was life-long friends with our father.) Living in Mexico was cheap, and Byron and Mike had little interest in work. They hung out, smoked weed, blended in, and learned the language. After a time they decided to utilize their agricultural skills along with their Mexican friends. You guessed it, they grew marijuana, acres of it. Labor was cheap. Everything was cheap. Byron and Mike became quite successful in this new venture. We heard neither hide nor hair from the boys for over a year.

One day in 1969 they decided it was time to return home. They figured they could retire on the profits from their crops. They hired a guy to build double paneled walls in that old Volkswagen van they had. They stuffed the walls with pounds of marijuana, 305 pounds to be exact. They had strategized as to which border-crossing would be safest.

They drove and smoked and drove and smoked and had a grand ol' time. The higher they got the more cavalier they became, and soon they abandoned the original plan and crossed at Nogales. This was a colossal mistake. The authorities stopped them and discovered the illegal contraband right away. (We thought the Mexicans may have fingered them, but we didn't know.) Luckily they were caught on the American side of the border. Had it been in Mexico we might have never seen them again.

Approaching the border

Leaving the border

Mike and Byron were arrested and held in the Nogales jail. Both fathers, Byron and Scotty, were called and did what they could to help. Scotty immediately bailed Mike out, to the tune of $10,000, pending trial. Pamela, our step mother, obstinately argued against posting bail for young Byron. Our father thought his political connections would do the trick, and he left his son in that jail while he tried to work his magic. He appealed to the US Senator, Thomas Kuchel, who was a moderate Republican from California. He was also the minority whip in the Senate. Byron had helped elect Senator Kuchel. He also reached out to State Senator Howard Way, a personal family friend. Our father was crushed to discover his connections did nothing to get his son out of trouble.

US Senator Thomas Kuchel with Lyndon Johnson

Eventually my brother was released into the legal custody of our father, pending trial. At this point, I was returning from overseas to settle down back home in Visalia. I thought I could breeze in and fix things. That fell flat. My brother was depressed, moody, and introverted. His grand plans had been dashed, and now he was under the thumb of his father. He was also furious at Pamela for opposing posting bail. He resisted every limit put upon him. Our father was fighting his own demons of political powerlessness. Both father and son were shut down. There was a relentless black cloud over all of us. The situation was grim.

Our father required Byron to work in the fields. The cotton was as high as the temperature. Chopping cotton was backbreaking work, and in 110 degrees it was god-awful. He was instructed to walk each row of cotton with a hoe and chop out every other plant and the weeds. Byron managed to convince our father to let another friend named Mike (Mike Cross) to come and work with him.

Many years later Mike told the story that the boys walked one row, sat under a tree and smoked a joint, then walked the next row and so on. They worked their way across the field all right, and collected pay at the end of the day. Of course the stipulations of the custody required "no use of illegal substances." Byron and Mike didn't let that bother them.

The wait seemed like forever, but the trial finally took place. The boys were tried separately. They were convicted of violation of the Stamp Tax Act of 1937, which required a payment of $100 tax on every ounce of marijuana – or face 5 years in prison and a stiff fine.

In 1969 Professor Timothy Leary challenged the Marijuana Stamp Tax law. It went all the way to the US Supreme Court, and he won. Since then states now use the current tax stamp laws to impose an additional penalty – tax evasion – not unlike what happened to Al Capone. You might remember good ol' Al was imprisoned for tax evasion, not prostitution or murder.

Marijuana stamp tax act of 1937

Because of the large amount of marijuana, 305 pounds, the case against them was much worse. Byron was convicted and sentenced to the federal prison in Lompoc. That facility has been described as the country-club prison, but believe me, no penitentiary bears any resemblance to a country club. On top of that he was given an indeterminant sentence, which means he had no clue as to when he might get out. It was up to the parole board each time it met. This type of sentence has since been thrown out. In the meantime Mike Wells was still out and walking the streets. It was just unfair. But later Mike had to serve his sentence.

The entrance to Lompoc Prison. Note the armed tower to the left.

I learned a lot about prisons and prison life when I visited my brother while he was there. For me it was terrifying. The big, heavy locked doors clanged, the guards stood in the towers brandishing machine guns, and our credentials were checked and rechecked. I was intimidated, and I wasn't even a prisoner. Prisons did not rehabilitate either. My brother had more education than the warden. What could they offer him in the way of rehabilitation?

There were rules, lots of them, but the unwritten rules were needed to survive. There were three distinct groups: the Hispanics, the Blacks, and the Whites. Those who crossed racial lines suffered.

Prison farms

There was work. My brother ended up as manager of the kitchen. He ordered food from the outside and coordinated the use of produce from the prison farm. After work there was time – lots of time – to fill. Some prisoners lifted weights, some read, some played dominos or cards, some just got in trouble. Byron took up duplicate bridge. He actually earned some master points while in prison. (Master points are awarded for scoring high in tournaments sanctioned by the American Bridge Association.)

Byron spent 18 months in Lompoc Penitentiary. Overall prison is an institution of fear. He had to remain hypervigilant at all times. He was never the same. That place changed him. He became uneasy, distrustful, and reclusive, and remained so for the rest of his life.

Byron's friend, Mike Wells, eventually served 18 months as a co-conspirator and he received the same sentence, even though his father, Scotty, bailed Mike out pending trial. Mike served his time at the prison in San Pedro, CA, sometime after Byron completed his sentence at Lompoc. Mike managed to get assigned to a work-release program while serving his time. During the day he had a job editing films in Hollywood. While the boys were in close proximity, contact of any kind was prohibited. In spite of the stress of this horrible situation, the friendship between Byron and Mike survived.

Byron returned to UCLA to complete his Masters in Public Administration after he was released in 1970. He found employment at The May Company as a night janitor, and he bunked in the UCLA dorms for the summer.

Maria Lanteri, the girl from Ipanema

My Dirty Dozen

Maria Lanteri arrived from Brazil to attend a language school at UCLA in January of 1971. She moved into the 17th floor of the dorms. Byron happened to be across the hall. It was in the cafeteria that Byron noticed this beautiful exotic girl who didn't speak English, but they didn't let that stand in the way. Since Maria was here to learn the language, she jumped at the opportunity to practice with this handsome California beach bum. From the time Byron laid eyes on Maria, he was not thinking English, that's for sure. *Baskin Robbins*™ was just around the corner and he found Maria's soft spot – rocky road ice cream. It worked much better than roses or chocolates. They became regulars at B/R-31. Maria had her own pronunciation. She was in love with "hocky hode" (use guttural H").

By the end of February Maria's Brazilian friends returned home, but she decided to stay and continue her studies. She found a tiny apartment on Weston Ave. and Wilshire Blvd. There was only room for a Murphy bed, but it had a view of the Hollywood sign from its one window. Rent was $110 a month, furnished. From then on Byron stayed in the dorm Monday – Friday and with Maria on weekends.

Maria Lanteri

Byron and Maria had no wheels. Our wheeler-dealer father found a rattle-trap blue Opel for $200. Dad drove the Opel and Pamela, his second wife, drove the pick-up to Los Angeles to deliver the car to the kids.

Then Byron and Maria came to Visalia in the summer of 1971. They stayed at our mother's house in Farmersville. It had plenty of room and a pool. I'm sure Mother was delighted to have her son home again. Byron went to work for our father in the peach orchard. Maria joined them in the heat, and the dust, and the itchy peach fuzz. Maria was accustomed to a life of privilege, and roughing it in the fields was not her idea of fun. After three days she walked off the job and into Mother's air-conditioned car.

At summer's end the kids high-tailed it back to LA. Byron completed his course work for his masters. By this time Maria's English was strong enough that she could to handle university classes. She enrolled as an Art History major at UCLA. Her friends, Illiana and Steven McKain, had a house in Santa Monica close to the campus. Since the McKains were out of the country, they let Maria and Byron stay there. Before long Maria found their own apartment in Santa Monica for only $160 a month, but it had no furniture. Back to Visalia they went, to pick up a truck full of hand-me-downs to furnish their new place. Their good friends Bill Arblaster and Mary Jane owned a small house in Venice Beach, California. They were living in Washington state at the time, so Byron and Maria moved into their house in Venice. When Bill and Mary Jane returned they squeezed everybody in that tiny house, where they stayed until 1974.

Byron found a job at a health food store in Los Angeles called *Erehwon* (Nowhere spelled backwards). This store was the pioneer of the health food industry. Because of his prison experience managing the kitchen, Byron became the manager of the *Erewhon* warehouse in Culver City, CA. He kept that position from 1971 – 1974. Soon Byron and Maria followed the trendy macrobiotic diet.

In the meantime I was married and teaching. I was looking for a class to take during my summer break and found a good one at Fresno State entitled "Working With Boys." Maria decided to take the class with me. It was a fun time commuting an hour each way together. Maria and I hit it off right away. Neither of us had trouble keeping the conversation going. We learned a little from that class, but more about each other. We are still close to this day.

Once Byron's parole obligation was fulfilled, he was free to leave the country. Off they went to Brazil in January,1974. At first they lived in Nova Friburgo, a flat near Ipanema Beach, in Rio de Janeiro, owned by Maria's mother. While it was inconveniently located, the price was right. They set up housekeeping and Byron proceeded to learn the language and absorb the culture.

Maria knew English now, but Byron didn't know Portuguese. Maria's mother and family were thrilled to meet Byron, a blonde haired, blue-eyed American. In Brazil the prime objective was to lighten the gene pool. It may not have been politically correct, but this was the truth. Picture this – the family was gathered for Sunday dinner and everyone was jabbering away in Portuguese. Byron had no clue, and nobody bothered to translate. So what was a guy to do? Maria's mother gave him an English/Portuguese dictionary. Other than that he was on his own. He sat there and smiled for a solid year. Until he got a handle on the language, he just smiled.

After two months Maria's brother and friends came to live at the flat in Nova Friburgo. This made it necessary for Maria and Byron to move to Nova Caledonia, in the mountains three hours outside of Rio. It was beautiful there with a great view. The rent was paid by Maria's mother, so all they were responsible for was power, butane, a gardener, and a maid. Byron's language skills improved to the point that he got a job. He worked for Maria's brother in a leather shop. They acquired a used VW bug, so they were able to get around and have some measure of independence.

When Maria became pregnant in June of 1974, she moved back to Rio with her mother in order to have access to proper medical care. Byron remained behind until November.

On February 13, 1975, they celebrated a new life. Temptation was to keep the family name and call him Byron William Jennings IV. My brother refused. He said, "I just can't do that to him. Being *the third* is hard enough." So we added Michael Lanteri Jennings to the family tree. We thought that he might be the reincarnation of his great-grandfather, Byron Jennings Sr., whose birthday was February 14. Michael was born by cesarean section just a few seconds before midnight on February 13th. He was blonde, and he was beautiful. Everyone was happy. He was a treasure to all of us.

My Dirty Dozen

Maria and the baby stayed with her mother for a year and a half. Finally Byron joined them in December. The young family lived three months together in Urca, Brazil, where they enjoyed a lovely view of Sugar Loaf Mountain.

Proud Papa with baby Michael, in Brazil

Byron, Maria and Michael in Brazil

In a couple of years the family decided to return to the United States. Of course young Michael spoke Portuguese and was certainly Brazilian by culture. So on the flight he expressed his two-year-old self by yelling in Portuguese "The plane is falling! The plane is falling!" much to the chagrin of his parents and all the passengers. (Remember Grandpa Fisher also believed airplanes would fall out of the air.)

Maria, Michael, Byron

They landed in California with only a few possessions and no place to live. At that time I was living in a small duplex on Garden Street in Visalia. Half of my duplex was vacant, so they moved in next door. Michael was two before I met him. I was thrilled. I treasured this time with my one and only nephew. He sat on my lap, and we read vocabulary picture books together.

According to the terms of the *fiance' visa*, Maria was required to get married within 90 days of entering the United States. They married on the 90th day, just under the wire.

I was in graduate school at the time working on my Master's in Social Work. This program required a lot of writing. Once I complained about this to my brother, and he said, "That's easy." I said "No it isnt!" Off we went into another of our famous arguments. But we simmered down, and he explained it to me. I didn't get his point right away. So when I was assigned the next reaction paper, we sat down and talked it through. He showed me how to 1) Tell them what you are going to say, (introduction) 2) Tell them, (body) 3) Tell them what you told them, (conclusion). He walked me through the process a couple of times and that was it. I became a writer. Thanks Byron. This joint effort did a lot to mend our relationship. For that I am most grateful.

Byron finally got a real job. He wore a suit and tie and gave lectures to doctors and dentists on how to invest their money overseas. He was well qualified for such a position, because he was a clever guy, well informed, and he was quick on his feet. It was strange to see him dressed up however. At the same time he travelled to UCLA once a month to work on his thesis and complete his Masters in Public Administration. He graduated with honors. His advisor highly recommended that he go to the east coast and get his Ph. D. Byron told him, "No, I have a family now. I am going to work with my father."

Old Hired Hand House on Farmersville Blvd.

I was disappointed when they moved out of my duplex into a house owned by our father. That little house was practically falling down, but again the price was right. I was shocked when my brother went to work for our father, because he had despised that work for decades. Our father was in seventh heaven because his son finally followed in his footsteps.

My Dirty Dozen

Strathmore house in Orange Grove

By that time our father had moved with Pamela into a small farm house in Strathmore, California, in the middle of his orange grove. This house came in handy for those frosty nights when they had to tend the smudge pots and later the wind machines to protect the oranges. We had many all-night parties while they watched over the trees.

The statute of limitations should have passed by now. I can reveal the contents of the hot house attached to their little house in that remote orange grove. You guessed it. They had marijuana – huge plants like small trees in pots under grow-lights. This was our father's project. We all knew he had a green thumb. You would have thought they had learned their lesson, but *no!* The hot house was covered and invisible from the air. Somehow they got away with it. It was not really a cash crop. It was more for personal use. Byron, both

Byrons, made liberal use of it, too. (In case you were wondering, pot was never my thing. I had nothing against it morally. For me, it was a social thing to do on rare occasions. It was never central to my life.)

Time marched on. Michael was in school doing well just like his daddy did. He loved baseball and as a south-paw, became a fine first baseman. Byron and Maria drifted apart and eventually divorced. During this period of time Byron and I had lengthy conversations as he worked through issues of divorce and custody. It was a contentious legal battle, but against common practice, Byron gained custody of Michael. People will tell you, and I agree, Byron was a most attentive father. Those two guys were as close as a father and son could be.

Father, Byron and son, Michael, always enjoying each other

Even though Byron had full custody, he generously shared parenting with Maria. Michael stayed with his mother in Visalia on a regular basis. They did a nice job of co-parenting. The arrangement was as seamless as it could be, considering the situation.

Byron purchased another home not far from our father's in Strathmore, also in an orange grove, and also remote. Michael transferred to Strathmore schools and later to Monache High School in Porterville, California.

Michael, 21, looking like his father

By then our father's health had declined and my brother took on more and more responsibility. In 1984 our father died, leaving the farming operation to his son. That was a difficult time for all concerned, but eventually we got through it.

My brother did a nice job of fixing up the two-story farm house in his orange grove in Strathmore. Byron was a good farmer and a great father. He attended all of Michael's games. He encouraged, supported, cajoled, and even pushed that boy. Michael turned into a fine young man. He enrolled in Cal Poly, San Luis Obispo, with a major in agri-business.

It was not possible for one man to keep up with all the chores of an active farm. Byron hired help when he needed it. He knew of a hired hand our father had employed at his place in Farmersville in the past. Byron contacted the worker and hired him, along with three of his friends, to help in his orange grove in Strathmore. He got to know these men as they worked together. When he found out they had also been incarcerated, he felt an affinity, and he wanted to give them a break. In time they became friendly.

Byron was now living alone in the house in the country, except when Michael came home for holidays. Byron became active in the community, joining the Chamber of Commerce and the Rotary Club. He befriended the neighbors. Mind you, neighbors are not all that close by in the country. Roger Bodine was the closest, about half mile across the grove.

Roger and his wife had invited Byron to dinner on the evening of February 5th, 1997. Byron looked forward to dinner with the Bodines. He was alone working at his computer. It was raining hard. There was a knock at the door. When he opened the door, there stood these ex cons, four of them. It was wet outside, and he let them in. Byron began to get the feeling this was not a neighborly call. Something was wrong. One man distracted Byron while the others scattered through the house. They seemed to be looking for something in the basement. Byron had no intention of allowing anybody to roam around his house. He told them in no uncertain terms, "Get the f*** out of my house." He tried to signal for help, but the alarm system had been disabled. He tried to call for help but the phone lines had been cut. He had a gun, but it was in the drawer and he couldn't reach it. There were four of them and only one of him. He was physically strong – even at 51 years of age. One of the men retrieved a tire iron from the trunk of the car. They overcame him and severely beat him with that tire iron. They smashed him over and over. He went down! He couldn't get up. He was severely injured and bled profusely. There were bloody streaks on either side of the doorway where he tried mightily to hang on, but slid to the floor. The rug was soaked with his blood.

There was a heavy safe in the basement, and we suspect they knew the contents of the safe, that contained gold and money for payroll. They hefted that unopened safe up the cellar steps and outside to their car in the rain. The four helped themselves what to whatever else they wanted in the house and left. Later the investigation revealed that safe had been opened and emptied and tossed into a dry river bed.

Roger and his wife wondered why Byron had missed their dinner date. They hadn't wanted to call too early the next morning. Once they noticed the commotion at the Jennings' place they came over and discovered the tragedy.

Finally in the afternoon Byron's bloody body was found rolled in a carpet under an orange tree.

The four thugs were convicted of murder and condemned to life. There were ten conspirators altogether. One of the assailants used Byron's credit card at WalMart in nearby Tulare. The clerk had a suspicious feeling when the customer escaped to the parking lot on the pretense of retrieving his I.D. She followed him outside and when he disappeared, she called the police and the bank. She was a good samaritan who helped catch some very bad guys. Another goon used Byron's credit card at a casino where there were surveillance cameras. The others were convicted of various charges: harboring fugitives, receiving stolen property, credit card fraud, and resisting arrest.

As a self-proclaimed bleeding-heart liberal, I assumed that every human had a nugget of gold somewhere inside. This disaster changed my mind. These savages possessed no redeeming social value. They did a monstrous thing, and they didn't care.

He was not a perfect man, but he didn't deserve this. It is hard to make sense of such a thing. My brother, Byron, was an intense, charismatic character. He was oh-so-smart, and he was funny. We laughed a lot, through the years. He was beautiful in appearance and in spirit. He did not deserve to be snuffed out. He had more to do, and he didn't get to complete his hopes and dreams. It just wasn't right.

How should I have handled such an unbearable loss? What was the right thing for me to do? How could I have best honored my brother? What would Byron have wanted?

I took time to decide. I didn't want to throw my own life away. I did not attend any of the trial. I decided not to dwell on the horror of it. I hold my brother in a private, holy place in my heart. And I am doing all I can to live my own best life. I think that is what he would have wanted.

Anytime you see me living large, you will know why.

I am honoring my serious, smart, sassy brother, Byron.

A truly exceptional individual.

Byron William Jennings III
(1946 – 1997)

The Last Word

A Family of Heroes

*

I reflect upon great-great-great grandpa, William Davis, who travelled over hill and dale, ridge and river, to establish the first white settlement on Indian Creek, Illinois, only to be slaughtered in 1832. I marvel at his courage and the drive and ambition to make a better life for his family.

Naysa Simmons and his wife, Sally, my great-great-great-great grandparents on Grandma Fisher's side, also travelled long distances to provide a better life for their family. Remember ol' Naysa who originated the Fountain Run Baptist Church in his Kentucky log cabin? The church allowed Naysa to remain in good standing in spite of the still in his back yard. He was defiant, yet he continually provided better circumstances for his people.

*Joseph Campbell. (n.d.). Retrieved August 7, 2016, from http://www.brainyquote.com/quotes/quotes/j/josephcamp138795.html

My Dirty Dozen

When I visualize Grandpa Jennings sitting tall and proud on his palomino, I remember his entrepreneurial spirit, purchasing Missouri Jack, and surviving the depression. As a teenager he worked his way through school. He tried out jobs such as teacher, telegrapher, and logger before settling into farming and horses and mules and wine and beer. He raised four fine children by himself after his wife's death.

I remember Grandpa Fisher as the strong silent type who rose above his many fears to show his love by building me a beautiful swing. He and Grandma were married for 55 years.

Grandma Fisher was sweet and soft. Her cranberry relish recipe is on the Ocean Spray™ package to this day. She devoted her very existence to Grandpa and her family.

My father, Byron, was the quintessential entertainer. He was always good for a great story. He was a man's man and a ladies' man and the life of every party.

Mother Mary fought the good fight year after year, refusing to surrender. She was a good wife and a fine mother, but she never received the glory.

Aunt Liz was never a mother, yet she was a first-class second mother to her sisters' children and me. She was opinionated, controversial, yet at the same time astute, refined, and divine.

Auntie Marge was nurturing in every sense of the word. Her cooking was good, and her hugs were better.

Aunts Geri and Thelma were both full of enthusiasm and the get-up-and-go needed to get 'er done.

Uncle Steve was loyal to a fault, and Aunt Mil always practical, productive, and persistent.

My brother, Byron, used his brilliance to think outside the box. He loved to play the odds and tempt fate. Sometimes he defied the odds; sometimes he didn't. I don't think he knew it, but everybody loved him.

It has been said that I come from a long line of compelling characters. This is something I cannot argue, and yet there is more. They were in my face and on my back and they pushed, and pushed hard. They commanded my attention. They asked me to change, to do more and be more. They gave me no choice. Maybe I didn't like, it but I did it anyway. They made me think and grow and become a better person. My family, each one, was a hero in my eyes. Remembering them has caused me to fall in love with them all over. I hope you feel the same.

(to be continued)

Get Back on That Horse, a memoir about growing up on a farm will be available sometime in 2017.

My Dirty Dozen

DUST, SWEAT, AND BLOOD

"It is not the critic who counts; not the man who points out how the strong man stumbles, or where the doer of deeds could have done them better. The credit belongs to the man who is actually in the arena, whose face is marred by dust and sweat and blood, who strives valiantly; who errs and comes short again and again; because there is not effort without error and shortcomings; but who does actually strive to do the deed; who knows the great enthusiasm, the great devotion, who spends himself in a worthy cause, who at the best knows in the end the triumph of high achievement and who at the worst, if he fails, at least he fails while daring greatly, so that his place shall never be with those cold and timid souls who know neither victory nor defeat."

Theodore Roosevelt

Acknowledgments

Writing a book was something I never thought I would do. Then I joined the Life Writing class only to jot down some of my father's stories. This class encouraged, cajoled, and buoyed me up week after week. My classmates did something for me I could never have done for myself. You lifted me up and made me a writer.

Let's not forget the great teachers who made an indelible mark upon me. Three come to mind. Mrs. Emma Goedeker, who recognized my struggle in grade-school, yet encouraged me at every opportunity; Mr. John Otto who promised me I was not dumb, and I would learn to read; Mr. Richard Bayard who valued my divergent way of thinking when nobody else did.

Two graphics designers deserve recognition. David Lutz formatted the book and brought my computer skills up to speed. Meri Rehman, from Pakistan, turned my verbal description into a map embellished with her charming art work.

Juliane McAdam patiently corrected every P and every Q. Lenny Erickson, the comma queen, straightened my warped grammar and fixed up my spelling. Ila June Bruener, Debbie Levi and I put our heads together and dug deep into the very soul and intention of our writings. Ours was a true collaboration. Laura Austin and my cousin, Joyce Stambaugh, both have praised me to high heaven. They kept me going.

What more can a girl ask? I am genuinely blessed.

Made in the USA
Las Vegas, NV
07 September 2023

77206082R00125